The New
Soul Food
Cookbook

The New Soul Food Cookbook

Healthier Recipes for Traditional Favorites

WILBERT JONES

CITADEL PRESS
Kensington Publishing Corp.
www.kensingtonbooks.com

CITADEL PRESS BOOKS are published by

Kensington Publishing Corp.
850 Third Avenue
New York, NY 10022

All Kensington titles, imprints, and distributed lines are available at special quantity discounts for bulk purchases for sales promotions, premiums, fund-raising, educational, or institutional use. Special book excerpts or customized printings can also be created to fit specific needs. For details, write or phone the office of the Kensington special sales manager: Kensington Publishing Corp., 850 Third Avenue, New York, NY 10022, attn: Special Sales Department; phone 1-800-221-2647.

CITADEL PRESS and the Citadel logo are Reg. U.S. Pat. & TM Off.

First printing: July 2005

10 9 8 7 6 5 4 3 2 1

Printed in the United States of America

Cataloging data may be obtained from the Library of Congress

ISBN 0-8065-2694-7

This book is dedicated
to the following people
who encouraged me to be
the best that I can be:

My grandmother, Ruth L. Randle *(in loving memory)*

My godmother, Shirley A. Fields *(in loving memory)*

My mentor, Tessie L. Garner

Contents

The Lowdown on Low Carbs

About ten years ago, I wrote *The New Soul Food Cookbook*. This was a time when low-fat, low-sodium, and low-cholesterol diets were popular with consumers, so my book was a reflection of that period. It showed readers how to cut back the fat, sodium, and cholesterol but keep the flavor.

Today, millions of Americans have incorporated some type of low-carb diet into their daily lives. Popular books and food and beverage products have saturated the stores—many following the patterns of *The Atkins Diet*, *The Zone Diet*, *The South Beach Diet*, *Protein Power Diet*, *Suzanne Somers's Diet* and *Sugar Busters!* Many professionals in the food and health-care industry believe that losing weight is not just about taking on a low-fat diet, but eating low-carb foods as well.

Carbohydrates are found in breads, cereal, pasta, rice, grains, fruits, vegetables, dairy products, and sugar. They are broken down into glucose, which the body uses for energy. If this stored glucose is not burned off through exercise, it will turn into stored fat, which causes weight gain—even with a low-fat diet.

To address the low-carb trend, I've provided some updated recipes containing fewer than 15 carbohydrate grams per serving—but still loaded with flavor.

Enjoy!

Introduction

African-American cooking—what most of us usually call soul food—has always been based on fresh country vegetables, a variety of meats, poultry, and fish, and the appeal of rich, irresistible desserts. An African-American table may be filled with such soul food staples as collard greens, ham hocks, corn bread, and sweet potato pie. The good news has always been that soul food is delicious, hearty, and laden with tradition. The bad news is that much of it is also laden with fat, cholesterol, sodium, and excess sugar. *The New Soul Food Cookbook* is all about keeping the good news and eliminating the bad. With everything we now know about how what we eat affects our health—and we seem to learn more every day—there is no reason to prepare traditional favorites in unhealthful ways.

Soul food originated in the slave quarters of Southern plantations. Simple ingredients were put to service in creating wonderfully complex flavors, such as combining the bitter and bland flavors of turnip greens, mustard greens, and spinach. And pork, for example, was a widely used ingredient because hogs were plentiful on plantations and grew fat very quickly. A lot of the creativity in African-American cooking relied on hogs, thus the abundance of smoked ham, pork chops, spare ribs, neck bones, pigs' feet, and lard on the soul food menu.

The preparation of traditional soul food has long been very labor intensive. Washing freshly picked greens or shelling fresh peas (let alone shopping for them) takes so much time that many African Americans no longer prepare soul food themselves on a regular basis and instead save it for holidays and special occasions like weddings or family reunions.

Today, fast food and prepared foods are the soul food shortcuts and substitutes. Some fast food restaurants offer cooked greens, corn muffins, macaroni and cheese, fried okra, and bread pudding. Grocery stores sell canned greens, bottled barbecue sauces, frozen fried chicken dinners, and dry corn bread mixes. All of that may sound terrific in terms of saving time and energy, but it is not so wonderful in terms of your health. Unfortunately, those fast food choices and store-bought foods are usually especially high in saturated fat, cholesterol, and sodium.

Soul food has all the good flavors that conjure warm memories and take us back to family celebrations. But let's face it, say nutritionists and food writers, this ethnic style of cooking can be life-threatening. African Americans are especially hard hit these days by heart disease, diabetes, and strokes. Health organizations such as the American Heart Association and the American Dietetic Association recommend that all Americans change their diets by eating more fruits, vegetables, and grains, and less fat and red meat. This cookbook offers you the chance to bring soul food within today's healthy eating guidelines by using more of the good, less or none of the bad, and a few healthy alternatives.

Each recipe in *The New Soul Food Cookbook* is a revised version of a traditional soul food recipe—I have trimmed fat, cholesterol, sodium, and sugar as much as possible. And, I admit that I am sorry to say, I have completely tossed certain unavoidably unhealthful foods such as pecan pie or anything made with chicken livers.

Throughout this cookbook I explain techniques that help you make a dish healthier, such as oven "frying" boneless, skinless chicken breasts; using your own freshly ground skinless turkey breast instead of the higher fat version of prepackaged ground turkey; and smoked turkey rather than pork to flavor old-fashioned dishes made with greens or beans.

Other techniques include substituting two egg whites for one whole egg (one large egg yolk has approximately 275mg of cholesterol and 2g of saturated fat, whereas egg whites contain no fat or cholesterol); using skim milk instead of whole milk (1 cup of whole milk contains 33mg of cholesterol and 5g of saturated fat, whereas skim milk has only 5mg of cholesterol and less than 1g of saturated fat); and using nonstick cooking spray instead of cooking oils, margarine, butter, or lard.

When preparing breads, rolls, cakes, or pies you should use nonstick bakeware to eliminate the fat used to grease the pans. For pies, you can use graham cracker crusts instead of traditional pastry crusts, which are usually loaded with butter or vegetable shortening. To add moisture to baked goods, ingredients like applesauce or mashed bananas are nonfat alternatives to oils.

Wherever possible, I suggest using nonstick cookware, usually with a light coat of nonstick cooking spray, such as Pam. This is an easy way to cut out the unwanted added fat from oils when cooking in a sauté pan or on a griddle. When frying with a little oil is a must, use canola oil, which has only 6 percent saturated fat.

I have also included recipes for healthful condiments, such as barbecue sauces, dips, and my all-purpose Soul Food Seasoning, which is an ingredient in many of the recipes here. These extras add a lot of taste to dishes that no longer have so much fat and sodium, those no-nos which used to provide much of the familiar flavors.

Most of the recipes here, in fact, contain little or no sodium. Traditional soul food recipes often have an abundance of salt, which can contribute to high blood pressure—a particular risk for many African Americans. High blood pressure, in turn, can lead to strokes. National health authorities recommend a daily intake of sodium no higher than 3,000mg per day. If you choose to add salt to your cooking, keep in mind that just one teaspoon of table salt contains about 2,000mg of sodium. Substitutions such as lemon or lime juice, vinegar, herbs, and spices are used throughout to perk up the flavors in these recipes.

At the end of each recipe is a nutritional profile for each serving or portion. Where a range of servings is given, the larger number is used for the analysis. Bear in mind that all the analyses are approximate, since precise weights of servings or amounts of fat or sodium in the ingredients will vary—and may vary further if ingredients are changed based on their availability or your preferences. But these numbers—for calories, fat, calories from fat, carbohydrates, protein, cholesterol, and sodium—provide a fairly accurate means toward following your own healthy eating plan. All the recipes were analyzed using Nutritionist IV, a software program that analyzes formulations, recipes, and food products.

Soul food has always nourished the soul. Now we can eat more of it—and eat it more often—knowing that we are nourishing our bodies as well. To give you ideas for planning full meals, particularly for special occasions, a selection of suggested menus precedes the recipes.

Suggested Menus

Early Morning Feast

Popovers
Baked Cheese Grits
Fried Yellow Squash with Zucchini
Spinach, Shrimp, and Eggs
Allspice Applesauce Cake

◆ ◆ ◆ ◆ ◆ ◆ ◆

Family Gathering
at Big Mama's

Pickled Okra
Pickled Cucumbers
Jalapeño Corn Bread
Classic Potato Salad
Cole Slaw
Hot Spaghetti with Ground Turkey
Lemon Pound Cake

◆ ◆ ◆ ◆ ◆ ◆ ◆

Mississippi
Traditional Dinner

Sweet Potato Chips
Unfried Hush Puppies
Black-Eyed Pea Salad
Unfried Skinless Chicken
Homemade Fries
Mississippi Dirty Rice
Mississippi Mud Cake

◆ ◆ ◆ ◆ ◆ ◆ ◆

Sunday Dinner

Sweet Potato Biscuits
Fried Green Tomatoes
Cucumber Salad
Smothered Chicken
Cream-Like Potatoes
Peach Cobbler
Jelly Cake
Iced Tea

◆ ◆ ◆ ◆ ◆ ◆ ◆

The New Soul Food Cookbook

Appetizers

Fried Okra

The season peak for okra is summer. Tender okra (bright green) is vital for this dish because it remains tender through the frying.

1 ½ pounds fresh okra
1 egg white
2 teaspoons freshly ground black
  pepper

1 teaspoon chili powder
½ cup cornmeal
nonstick cooking spray

Wash and dry the okra (if there are any stems on the okra, cut them off). In a large bowl, beat egg white well and mix in the black pepper and chili powder. Toss the okra in the egg white mixture, coating each piece well. Remove the okra and roll in the cornmeal. Spray some cooking spray in a hot cast-iron skillet. Place the okra in the skillet and cook on each side for 5 to 7 minutes (or until it turns brown). Makes about 15 to 20 pieces. *Serves 8.*

Nutritional information per piece:

calories = 25
sodium = 7mg
calories from fat = 3

carbohydrate = 5g
protein = 1g

cholesterol = 0mg
fat = <1g

Fried Green Tomatoes

A few dashes of Louisiana Hot Sauce can be used instead of lemon juice to give these fried green tomatoes a spicier flavor.

6 large green tomatoes (about 3 pounds)

2 tablespoons lemon juice

½ cup cornmeal

2 teaspoons freshly ground black pepper

nonstick cooking spray

Slice each tomato into 1/2-inch-thick slices. Sprinkle the lemon juice on the tomatoes. Mix the cornmeal and black pepper in a plastic bag. Put the tomato slices into the bag and shake well. Coat a cast-iron skillet or nonstick sauté pan with nonstick cooking spray. Fry the tomatoes, over medium-high heat, until they are light brown on each side. *Serves 4.*

Nutritional information per serving:

calories = 105	carbohydrate = 22g	cholesterol = 0mg
sodium = 22mg	protein = 3g	fat = 2g
calories from fat = 16		

Fried Bananas

This appetizer can be served with a nonfat cottage cheese or with a Nonfat Cucumber Dip or Nonfat Spinach Dip (see pages 124 and 125). For something less sweet, use plantains instead of bananas.

4 yellow bananas   *nonstick cooking spray*

Peel and cut the bananas lengthwise into 1/4-inch thick slices. Spray some nonstick cooking spray in a nonstick skillet and add the bananas. Cook each side of the banana for about 2 to 3 minutes on a medium heat or until both sides turn brown. *Serves 4.*

Nutritional information per serving:

calories = 110   carbohydrate = 27g   cholesterol = 0mg
sodium = 1mg   protein = 1g   fat = 1g
calories from fat = 7

Sweet Potato Chips

This snack tastes great with Nonfat Cucumber Dip (see page 124).

3 pounds large sweet potatoes
(about 5)
2 tablespoons Soul Food Seasoning
(see page 123)

2 egg whites, lightly beaten
nonstick cooking spray

Preheat oven to 400°F. Clean and scrub the sweet potatoes thoroughly. Peeling the potatoes before slicing them is optional. Using a sharp knife or automatic slicer, slice the sweet potatoes about 1/8-inch thick. Place the sliced potatoes in a large bowl; sprinkle with the soul food seasoning and pour in the egg whites. Stir to coat all the slices evenly. Spread the potatoes on a nonstick baking sheet (lightly coated with nonstick cooking spray) in a single layer. Do not allow the potatoes to overlap or else they will stick together. Spray the potatoes with nonstick cooking spray 2 times. Bake for about 40 minutes (turning them over every 10 minutes) or until crispy. *Serves 6.*

Nutritional information per serving:

calories = 190
sodium = 41mg
calories from fat = 7

carbohydrates = 43g
protein = 4g

cholesterol = 0mg
fat = 1g

Pickled Cucumbers

A beautifully arranged platter of pickled cucumbers and okra is attractive and especially delectable when served with a Nonfat Spinach Dip (see page 125).

*2 pounds kirby (pickling)
    cucumbers (about 10)*
4 cloves garlic, peeled

1 ½ pint distilled white vinegar
2 sprigs fresh dill
2 sprigs fresh tarragon

Wash and dry the cucumbers. Place 2 cloves of garlic in each of 2 hot sterilized canning jars. Divide the cucumbers between the 2 jars. In a saucepan, bring the vinegar to a boil. Pour the hot vinegar over the cucumbers in the jars and add equal amounts of dill and tarragon. Let the jars cool to room temperature. Seal with sterilized lids. Let the jars set for 3 to 4 weeks in the refrigerator before opening and eating. *Makes about 2 quarts.*

Nutritional information per pickled cucumber:

calories = 20	carbohydrate = 6g	cholesterol = 0mg
sodium = 3mg	protein = 1g	fat = <1g
calories from fat = 1		

Pickled Okra

This appetizer can be eaten with a salsa or sweet hot pepper sauce.

1 pound fresh okra (about 8 to 10 pieces)
2 cloves garlic, peeled

2 cups distilled white vinegar
1 sprig fresh dill
2 jalapeño peppers

Wash and dry the okra. Place the garlic in a sterilized one-quart canning jar. In a saucepan over high heat, bring the vinegar to boiling. Pour the hot vinegar over the okra in the jar. Put the dill and jalapeño peppers in the jar and let cool until it reaches room temperature. Seal the jar with a clean sterilized lid. Let the jar set for 4 to 5 weeks in the refrigerator before opening and eating. *Makes 1 quart.*

Nutritional information per pickled okra:

calories = 25
sodium = 18mg
calories from fat = 1

carbohydrate = 6g
protein = 1g

cholesterol = 0mg
fat = <1g

Baked Cheese Grits

This appetizer can be served hot or cold and can be served with a hot or mild salsa.

1 cup uncooked grits
½ teaspoon reduced-fat margarine
3 egg whites, lightly beaten

¼ cup grated reduced-fat cheddar
  cheese
1 teaspoon finely minced garlic

Preheat oven to 350°F. Bring 4 cups of water to a boil in a medium saucepan over high heat. Stir in the grits and reduce heat, cooking until they become thick, about 10 minutes. Stir in the margarine, egg whites, cheese, and garlic, mixing thoroughly. Pour the mixture into a 9-inch nonstick pie pan and bake 40 to 50 minutes, or until lightly browned on the top. Remove from oven and cool in pan on wire rack. When grits cool, cut into small squares or diamonds, or use a cookie cutter for unusual shapes. *Serves 4.*

Nutritional information per serving:

calories = 75
sodium = 234mg
calories from fat = 20

carbohydrate = 9g
protein = 6g

cholesterol = 5mg
fat = 2g

African-American Meatballs

These meatballs substitute ground turkey breast for ground beef, which cuts down on a lot of the fat and cholesterol found in traditional recipes. Instead of buying pre-ground turkey at the supermarket, buy fresh skinless turkey breast and grind it yourself in a meat grinder or food processor. This guarantees that you will be using the leanest meat possible. Herbal Barbecue Sauce (see page 122) is a tasty complement to these spicy meatballs.

*1 cup whole wheat bread crumbs
  (toast and crumble your own
  whole wheat bread — store-bought
  bread crumbs are high in fat)
1 tablespoon minced onion
2 teaspoons freshly ground black
  pepper*

*1 pound ground turkey breast
3 egg whites, lightly beaten
3 tablespoons Louisiana Hot Sauce
2 tablespoons ketchup
1 teaspoon prepared horseradish
nonstick cooking spray*

Mix the bread crumbs, onion, and black pepper together well in a large bowl. Add the ground turkey breast, egg whites, hot sauce, ketchup, and horseradish. Using your hands, mix thoroughly. Cover the mixture with plastic wrap and refrigerate for 4 to 5 hours so that the flavors can blend. Shape the mixture into 12 to 15 1 1/2-inch balls.

Preheat oven to 375°F. Lightly coat a baking sheet with nonstick cooking spray. Place the meatballs on the baking sheet and bake for about 40 minutes or until the meatballs are firm and no longer pink on the inside. *Serves 6 as an appetizer.*

Nutritional information per meatball:

calories = 50	carbohydrate = 2g	cholesterol = 19mg
sodium = 63mg	protein = 8g	fat = 1g
calories from fat = 10		

Stuffed Mushrooms Wrapped in Turkey Bacon

Freshly diced vegetables (such as carrots or green peppers) can also be sautéed and stuffed inside these mushroom caps before wrapping them with turkey bacon.

½ cup diced onion
6 ounces sliced smoked turkey bacon

nonstick cooking spray
½ pound fresh white mushrooms

Sauté the onion in a nonstick skillet sprayed with cooking spray for about 5 minutes or until translucent. Stir constantly so that the onion does not burn (use more cooking spray if necessary). Set aside. Cut each piece of turkey bacon in half (about 3 to 4 inches long). Wash and dry the mushrooms and remove the stems from the caps by gently twisting them. Stuff the mushroom caps with some of the sautéed onion. Preheat oven to 400°F. Roll each piece of turkey bacon around a mushroom cap and stick a toothpick in the center to hold together while baking. Bake in a nonstick roasting pan for 25 minutes or until the turkey bacon is evenly brown. *Makes about 12 to 15 mushrooms, depending on the size.*

Nutritional information per mushroom:

calories = 26	carbohydrate = 1g	cholesterol = 8mg
sodium = 138mg	protein = 4g	fat = 2g
calories from fat = 15		

Tuna Pâté

This appetizer is very easy to make and can be served cold, sliced or spread on toasted French bread or crackers. If fresh tuna is not available, canned tuna (solid white, packed in water, drained) can be used as a substitute.

1 pound fresh solid tuna or canned, solid white tuna packed in water and drained
2 egg whites
¼ cup finely chopped fresh green onion (scallions)

2 teaspoons ground white pepper
1 teaspoon chopped fresh dill
1 teaspoon chopped fresh tarragon
⅓ cup dry white wine

Preheat oven to 375°F. Place the tuna in a food processor and process briefly, until it breaks up into small chunks. Place the tuna in a bowl and mix the egg whites, onion, pepper, dill, tarragon, and wine with a wooden spoon. Place the mixture in a small baking pan and cover with foil. Bake for 40 to 45 minutes or until the tuna is brown and firm. Once the pâté is cool, place it in an air-tight container and refrigerate for about 4 hours before serving (this helps the flavors blend together). It will keep up to 3 days in the refrigerator. *Serves 4.*

Nutritional information per serving:

calories = 170	carbohydrate = 2gm	cholesterol = 40mg
sodium = 75mg	protein = 33g	fat = 2g
calories from fat = 20		

Baked Chicken Strips

4 boneless, skinless chicken breast
    halves
2 tablespoons fresh lemon juice
½ cup whole wheat bread crumbs
    (toast whole wheat bread and
    crumble)

½ cup of nonfat Parmesan cheese
    topping
1 tablespoon coarsely chopped fresh
    cilantro
½ teaspoon chopped fresh thyme
nonstick cooking spray

Preheat oven to 400°F. Cut the chicken breasts into approximately 1-inch-wide strips. Sprinkle lemon juice over chicken. In a bowl, mix together the bread crumbs, Parmesan, cilantro, and thyme. Roll each strip in the bread crumbs and coat well. Lightly coat a baking sheet with nonstick cooking spray. Place coated chicken strips on sheet and spray lightly. Bake for 20 to 30 minutes turning once or until crispy on both sides. *Serves 6.*

Nutritional information per serving:

calories = 200	carbohydrate = 8g	cholesterol = 95mg
sodium = 161mg	protein = 33g	fat = 4g
calories from fat = 32		

Breads, Rolls, and Biscuits

Jalapeño Corn Bread

Jalapeño peppers in corn bread will not only add an unexpected hot flavor to the sweet cornmeal, but will give each square or muffin a mix of yellow and green.

nonstick cooking spray
2 cups yellow cornmeal
1 cup all-purpose flour
2 ½ teaspoons baking powder
1 tablespoon sugar

2 diced fresh jalapeño peppers,
* seeded and chopped*
1 cup skim milk
6 egg whites
¼ cup cider vinegar

Preheat oven to 375°F. Lightly coat a 9½ x 9½-inch baking pan or 12-cup muffin pan with nonstick cooking spray. Mix the cornmeal, flour, baking powder, and sugar together in a large bowl. Add the peppers, milk, egg whites, and vinegar. Stir with a spoon until thoroughly mixed. Spoon the batter into the prepared pan. Bake 45 to 50 minutes or until the top of the corn bread is firm and light brown on the top. Cool in pan on wire rack. *Serves 6.*

Nutritional information per serving:

calories = 200	carbohydrate = 39g	cholesterol = 1mg
sodium = 130mg	protein = 8g	fat = 1g
calories from fat = 13		

Long Lost Hobo Bread

Long Lost Hobo Bread, also called Po Man's Bread, is so named because its ingredients are simple and almost always easy to find. Similar to potato pancakes, this bread can be served as an appetizer and eaten with applesauce or apple butter.

1 1/3 cups yellow cornmeal
1/4 cup shredded uncooked white
   potatoes, peeled
1 teaspoon baking powder
2 cups skim milk

1 tablespoon lemon juice
2 egg whites, lightly beaten
2 tablespoons chopped fresh green
   onions (scallions)
nonstick cooking spray

In a large bowl, combine the cornmeal, potatoes, and baking powder. Add the milk and lemon juice. Stir in the egg whites and scallions. Spoon about 2 tablespoons of batter into a hot nonstick skillet lightly coated with nonstick cooking spray. Cook on each side for 2 minutes or until brown. *Makes about 12 bread patties.*

Nutritional information per patty:
calories = 80
sodium = 260mg
calories from fat = 4

carbohydrate = 15g
protein = 3g

cholesterol = 1mg
fat = <1g

Molasses Bread

This sweet, rich-tasting bread is as good cold as it is hot, and it's perfect for breakfast.

nonstick cooking spray
2 ½ cups all-purpose flour
2 teaspoons baking powder
1 cup mashed banana

½ cup molasses
1 ½ cups skim milk, room
   temperature
4 egg whites, lightly beaten

Lightly coat a 8 x 4-inch loaf pan with nonstick cooking spray; set aside. In a large mixing bowl, combine the flour, baking powder, mashed banana, and molasses. Mix the ingredients with an electric mixer (on medium speed) for about 3 to 4 minutes or until the dough is smooth. Stir in the milk and egg whites with a spoon for about 1 minute. Preheat oven to 375°F. Pour the dough into the prepared pan and let stand for about 10 minutes before baking. Bake 40 to 50 minutes or until the center of the bread is brown and firm. Remove from pan and cool on wire rack. *Makes about 10 servings.*

Nutritional information per serving:

calories = 200	carbohydrate = 41g	cholesterol = 1mg
sodium = 123mg	protein = 6g	fat = <1g
calories from fat = 4		

Skillet Corn Bread

This version of corn bread is a nice change from the baked variety, and it can be eaten as a main dish for breakfast if it is served with some fresh fruit, fruit spread, or warm molasses.

½ cup yellow cornmeal
1 cup all-purpose flour
1 tablespoon granulated sugar
3 egg whites, lightly beaten

¾ cup skim milk
1 tablespoon nonfat sour cream
2 tablespoons chopped onion
nonstick cooking spray

In a large bowl, mix the cornmeal, flour, and sugar together. Stir in the egg whites, milk, sour cream, and onion. Lightly coat a medium skillet with nonstick cooking spray. Preheat the skillet over a low-medium heat. Pour about 3 tablespoons of batter into the skillet and cook on low heat for about 6 minutes, or until the tops are bubbly and undersides are golden brown. Turn and cook 6 minutes longer or until turns golden brown. *Serves 4.*

Nutritional information per serving:

calories = 140	carbohydrate = 27g	cholesterol = 1mg
sodium = 200mg	protein = 6g	fat = 1g
calories from fat = 5		

Sweet Potato Bread

If desired, a deeper shade of orange can be obtained by adding 1/2 teaspoon of orange food coloring to the batter before baking.

1 tablespoon reduced-fat margarine
2 tablespoons sugar
1 cup mashed sweet potatoes
1 ½ cup all-purpose flour
1 teaspoon ground cinnamon

1 teaspoon grated nutmeg
1 teaspoon baking soda
2 teaspoons vanilla extract
3 egg whites, lightly beaten

With an electric mixer, beat the margarine, sugar, and sweet potatoes together until light and fluffy. Add the flour, cinnamon, nutmeg, baking soda, and vanilla. Stir in the egg whites and mix well. Preheat oven to 350°F. Pour the batter into an 8 x 4-inch nonstick loaf pan, and let it set for 10 minutes in a warm place (about 85° F). Bake about 60 to 70 minutes or until the top is brown and the center is firm. Remove from pan to cool on wire rack. *Serves 10.*

Nutritional information per serving:

calories = 130
sodium = 68mg
calories from fat = 8

carbohydrate = 26g
protein = 4g

cholesterol = 0mg
fat = 1g

Tomato Bread

Herbs such as parsley or basil can be added to this recipe. Grated low-fat cheese, such as cheddar or Colby, can also be folded into the dough before baking.

1 package active dry yeast
½ cup warm water, 110°F.
1 cup cubed tomatoes (about 2 medium)

1 tablespoon sugar
1 tablespoon caraway seeds
3 cups unbleached white flour
1 egg white

Combine yeast and warm water. Place the tomatoes in a blender or food processor and whirl on high speed until completely liquified. Stir together the blended tomato, sugar, and caraway seeds in a large bowl. Stir in the flour vigorously and then the yeast mixture. Knead the dough on a floured surface for about 5 minutes. Place the dough back into the bowl, cover with plastic wrap, and let it rise until it doubles in size (about 1 hour). Preheat oven to 375°F. Put the dough in a non-stick 9 x 5-inch loaf pan. Brush the top of the dough with egg white (this creates a nice shine). Bake for about 45 minutes or until bottom sounds hollow when thumped with fingers. Remove from pan and cool on wire rack before slicing. *Serves 10.*

Nutritional information per serving:

calories = 155
sodium = 9mg
calories from fat = 9

carbohydrate = 32g
protein = 5g

cholesterol = 0mg
fat = 1g

Unfried Hush Puppies

Hush puppies are usually served with fish 'n' chips. However, a typical traditional Friday night dinner in many African-American homes consists of hush puppies, catfish, spaghetti, and cole slaw. These unfried hush puppies are a great, healthy alternative to deep-fried hush puppies.

nonstick cooking spray
1 ½ cups yellow cornmeal
¼ cup self-rising flour
2 ½ teaspoons baking powder
1 tablespoon sugar
½ teaspoon salt

½ cup chopped onion
2 tablespoons chopped fresh parsley
2 cups skim milk
1 egg white, lightly beaten
½ cup water

Preheat oven to 400°F. Lightly coat an 18-cup muffin pan with nonstick cooking spray. Mix the cornmeal, flour, baking powder, sugar, and salt together. Fold in the onion, parsley, milk, egg white, and water. Pour the batter into the prepared muffin pan filling each 3/4 full. Bake 20 to 25 minutes or until golden brown. *Makes 18 hush puppies.*

Nutritional information per hush puppy:

calories = 60
sodium = 272mg
calories from fat = 3

carbohydrate = 12g
protein = 2g

cholesterol = 0mg
fat = <1g

Nonfat, Cholesterol-Free Pancakes

Fresh blueberries or sliced bananas (about 1/2 cup each) can be added to this pancake batter before cooking. Serve the pancakes with a low-calorie syrup or top with fresh fruit.

2 cups all-purpose flour
1 tablespoon sugar
1 teaspoon baking powder
1 teaspoon ground cinnamon

¾ cup skim milk
3 egg whites, lightly beaten
nonstick cooking spray

In a large bowl, mix the flour, sugar, baking powder, and cinnamon. In a separate bowl, lightly beat the milk and egg whites. Add the liquid to the dry ingredients and stir well with a large spoon until thoroughly mixed. Pour about 3 tablespoons of batter for each pancake on a hot nonstick griddle or skillet lightly coated with nonstick cooking spray. *Makes about 8 medium-size pancakes.*

Nutritional information per pancake:

calories = 79	carbohydrate = 15g	cholesterol = 0mg
sodium = 74mg	protein = 4g	fat = <1g
calories from fat = 2		

Although this recipe calls for oregano, rosemary, and basil, other combinations of herbs can be used such as cilantro, chives, and marjoram.

1 package active dry yeast
½ cup warm water, 110°F.
2 ½ cups all-purpose flour
1 tablespoon sugar
½ teaspoon chopped fresh oregano
½ teaspoon chopped fresh rosemary
½ teaspoon chopped fresh basil

1 ⅓ cups cool water
2 egg whites, lightly beaten
½ cup reduced-fat margarine (cut
into small pieces)
nonstick cooking spray

Dissolve the yeast in the warm water. In a large bowl, mix the flour, sugar, oregano, rosemary, and basil together. Add the 1 1/3 cup water, dissolved yeast, egg whites, and margarine. Knead the dough for about 3 minutes. Cover it with plastic wrap and let it rise in a warm place (about 85°F.) until it doubles in size, about 1 to 1 1/2 hours. Preheat oven to 400°F. Lightly coat a baking sheet with nonstick cooking spray. Roll the dough out to about 1/3-inch thickness on a floured board. Using a biscuit cutter cut the rolls and put them on the baking sheet. Bake 20 to 25 minutes or until light brown. *Makes about 2 dozen rolls.*

Nutritional information per roll:

calories = 70	carbohydrate = 11g	cholesterol = 0mg
sodium = 51mg	protein = 2g	fat = 2g
calories from fat = 19		

Popovers

Instead of eating these favorites with butter or margarine, try them with fruit spreads or apple butter.

1 cup all-purpose flour
¼ teaspoon salt
1 tablespoon reduced-fat margarine

1 cup skim milk
4 egg whites, lightly beaten
nonstick cooking spray

Using an electric mixer, blend the flour, salt, and margarine together. Add the milk and egg whites, and mix until all ingredients are well blended. Preheat the oven at 450°F. and lightly coat a nonstick popover pan with nonstick cooking spray. Fill the popover cups halfway and bake at 450°F. for 20 minutes, then reduce the heat to 375°F. and bake for another 20 minutes. To check for doneness, remove one popover from the pan, touch, and see if the walls are firm (they should be); if not, the popover will collapse. Serve immediately. *Makes about 10 popovers.*

Nutritional information per popover:
calories = 70
sodium = 102mg
calories from fat = 7

carbohydrate = 11g
protein = 4g

cholesterol = 0mg
fat = 1g

Low-Fat Cheese Biscuits

Using a low-fat Monterey Jack or Colby cheese for these biscuits keeps them on the healthier soul food menu. You can add about 1 teaspoon of caraway seeds to this recipe to make Caraway Cheese Biscuits.

1 cup skim milk
1 package active dry yeast
2 ½ cups all-purpose flour

1 teaspoon baking powder
1 cup grated low-fat cheddar cheese
nonstick cooking spray

Heat the skim milk in a saucepan until it turns lukewarm. Dissolve the yeast in the milk. Sift the flour and baking powder into a large bowl. Stir the skim milk and cheese into the flour, then knead for about 3 minutes. Lightly coat a baking sheet with nonstick cooking spray. Roll the dough out to 1/2-inch thickness on a lightly floured board and cut with a biscuit cutter. Place the biscuits on the baking sheet. Let the biscuits stand at room temperature for about 25 minutes before baking. Meanwhile, preheat oven to 425°F. Bake the biscuits for about 20 minutes or until brown. *Makes about 18 biscuits, depending on the size of the biscuit cutter.*

Nutritional information per serving:

calories = 80
sodium = 72mg
calories from fat = 2

carbohydrate = 14g
protein = 4g

cholesterol = 0mg
fat = <1g

Sweet Potato Biscuits

These biscuits can be eaten with a little reduced-fat margarine or fruit spreads.

nonstick cooking spray
2 cups all-purpose flour
2 teaspoons baking powder
1 tablespoon granulated sugar
¼ teaspoon salt
1 tablespoon reduced-fat margarine

1 cup mashed sweet potato
½ teaspoon ground cinnamon
½ teaspoon grated nutmeg
1 cup skim milk
1 egg white

Preheat oven to 400°F. Lightly coat a baking sheet with nonstick cooking spray. Using an electric mixer, combine the flour, baking powder, sugar, salt, and margarine. Then slowly mix in the sweet potatoes, cinnamon, nutmeg, and milk. Stir in the egg white. On a lightly floured board, roll the dough out to 1/2-inch thickness. Using a biscuit cutter, cut the dough into 2-inch circles and place them on the baking sheet. Bake about 25 minutes or until they are firm in the center. *Makes about 14.*

Nutritional information per biscuit:
calories = 100
sodium = 290mg
calories from fat = 3
carbohydrate = 20g
protein = 3g
cholesterol = 0mg
fat = <1g

For yellow rice bread, add 1/2 teaspoon turmeric. For green rice bread, add 1/4 cup cooked, chopped spinach.

¼ cup reduced-fat margarine   *1 cup cooked rice*
2 egg whites at room temperature   *¾ cup all-purpose flour*
½ cup skim milk   *1 teaspoon baking powder*

Preheat the oven to 400°F. Melt the margarine in a 6-inch, nonstick pie pan. In a blender, blend the egg whites, milk, and rice for 30 seconds or until almost smooth. Add the flour and baking powder and continue to blend for 1 minute or until well mixed. Pour the batter into the pie pan and bake for 30 minutes or until it turns golden brown. Remove the bread from the oven and let it cool for 5 minutes. Cut into wedges and serve warm with reduced-fat margarine or fruit preserves. *Makes 6 servings.*

Nutritional information per serving:

calories = 142   carbohydrate = 21g   cholesterol = 0mg
sodium = 186mg   protein = 5g   fat = 4g
calories from fat = 37

Soups and Salads

Black Bean Soup

This version of black bean soup is made without the traditional flavoring of pork. However, adding a slice or two of smoked turkey bacon or skinless smoked chicken or turkey to the soup as it cooks will provide some of the complexity of flavor you give up when you leave out smoked ham hocks.

½ cup diced celery
½ cup diced onion
2 tablespoons crushed fresh garlic
nonstick cooking spray
3 cups dried black beans, rinsed
* and sorted*

1 teaspoon celery salt
1 teaspoon chili powder
¼ teaspoon ground red pepper
½ cup dry white wine
2 teaspoons Tabasco sauce

Over medium-low heat, sauté the celery, onion, and garlic for about 10 minutes (or until the vegetables become transluscent) in a nonstick skillet sprayed with nonstick cooking spray. Pour the beans, celery salt, chili powder, red pepper, wine, and Tabasco sauce in a large pot. Add the sautéed celery, onions, and garlic to the pot along with 12 cups of water. Over high heat, heat to boiling. Cover the pot, reduce heat to low, simmer for about 3 hours, stirring occasionally. *Makes 8 cups.*

Nutritional information per cup:

calories = 110
sodium = 19mg
calories from fat = 5

carbohydrate = 18g
protein = 6g

cholesterol = 0g
fat = 1g

Cabbage Soup

This soup is similar to Asian versions of cabbage soup. However, Asian cabbage soups usually include salt pork. This recipe calls for skinless smoked turkey breast.

1 pound finely chopped green cabbage
½ cup diced onion
1 teaspoon ground white pepper

1 teaspoon chopped fresh thyme
½ cup diced skinless smoked turkey breast

Place all the ingredients in a pot with 8 cups of water. Over high heat, heat to boiling. Reduce heat to low, cover, and cook for about 1 hour over a medium heat. *Makes about 9 cups.*

Nutritional information per cup:

calories = 30
sodium = 100mg
calories from fat = 3

carbohydrate = 3g
protein = 3g

cholesterol = 2mg
fat = <1g

Spinach Soup

If fresh spinach is not available, two 10-ounce packages of frozen spinach is a good substitute.

2 pounds fresh spinach
½ cup chopped onion
¼ cup chopped cooked smoked turkey
  bacon

1 teaspoon crushed red pepper flakes
1 teaspoon ground celery powder
1 cup skim milk

Wash the spinach thoroughly (make sure all the dirt and sand has been removed) and remove excess stems. Place the spinach, onion, and turkey bacon in a food processor or blender and chop for 2 minutes. In a large pot combine 4 cups of water, the red pepper, and ground celery. Bring to a boil and continue boiling for about 10 minutes. Add the spinach mixture and milk and cook another 15 minutes over medium heat. *Makes about 6 cups.*

Nutritional information per cup:
calories = 80
sodium = 270mg
calories from fat = 16

carbohydrate = 11g
protein = 8g

cholesterol = 7mg
fat = 2g

Tomato Soup

Tomato soup can be eaten hot during the winter months and served cold in the summer. Garnish with chopped scallions or sprigs of fresh dill.

5 cups fresh tomatoes, skinned and seeded
¼ cup chopped celery
¼ cup chopped onion

⅓ cup skim milk
1 tablespoon brown sugar
1 teaspoon chopped chives
½ cup water

Blend the tomatoes in a blender for about 2 minutes. Then combine the tomatoes with the celery, onion, milk, sugar, chives, and water in a pot and cook for 10 minutes or until it simmers. *Makes about 6 cups.*

Nutritional information per cup:

calories = 40	carbohydrate = 8g	cholesterol = 0mg
sodium = 21mg	protein = 1g	fat = <1g
calories from fat = 3		

Potato Carrot Soup

Some nonfat Parmesan cheese topping or unsalted nonfat cracker crumbs can be sprinkled on top of this soup, which can be served either hot or chilled.

6 white potatoes, peeled and diced
   (about 7 cups)
2 cups carrots, peeled and diced
2 cups diced onions
½ teaspoon celery seeds

½ teaspoon dried marjoram
2 ½ cups skim milk
1 teaspoon freshly ground black
   pepper
½ teaspoon crushed red pepper flakes

In a large pot, bring 6 cups of water to a boil. Add the potatoes, carrots, onions, celery seeds, and marjoram, and cook, covered, for about 20 minutes or until the vegetables are very soft. Drain the vegetables, careful to reserve about 4 cups of the liquid (this will be used as stock water later). Put the vegetables in a food processor and mix until smooth. Pour the milk and 3 cups of the reserved stock into a pot and bring to a boil. Add the vegetables along with the black pepper and crushed red pepper. Cook for about 5 minutes. Add more stock for a thinner soup. *Serves 10.*

Nutritional information per serving:

calories = 155
sodium = 46mg
calories from fat = 3

carbohydrate = 33g
protein = 6g

cholesterol = 1mg
fat = <1g

Cream of Lettuce Soup

Instead of tarragon, fresh cilantro and a dash of salsa can be used to create a southwestern flavor.

3 heads Boston lettuce
½ teaspoon freshly ground black
*   pepper*
1 tablespoon chopped fresh
*   tarragon*
nonstick cooking spray

½ cup plain nonfat yogurt
2 tablespoons freshly squeezed
*   lemon juice*
1 teaspoon Tabasco sauce
*   (optional)*

Wash the lettuce, remove the cores, and cut the heads into quarters. Boil the lettuce with 4 1/2 cups of water for about 15 minutes. Remove the lettuce from the pot, reserving liquid. Place the lettuce, black pepper, and tarragon in a medium saucepan sprayed with cooking spray. Cover and cook on low heat for about 3 minutes. Add reserved liquid; bring to a boil. Lower the heat and simmer (partially covering the pan) for about 45 minutes. Cool and puree in a blender or food processor. Pour the soup back into the saucepan and stir in the yogurt, lemon juice, and Tabasco sauce over low heat until heated through. *Serves 4.*

Nutritional information per serving:

calories = 40	carbohydrate = 6g	cholesterol = 1mg
sodium = 36mg	protein = 4g	fat = 1g
calories from fat = 6		

Black and White Bean Salad

For a more colorful and flavorful presentation, chopped, blanched broccoli, cauliflower, and carrots can be added to this recipe.

1 ½ cups cooked black beans
1 ½ cups cooked white beans (such as navy or cannelloni beans)
½ cup diced white onion
½ teaspoon salt

1 teaspoon freshly ground black pepper
1 cup diced green bell peppers
2 tablespoons sweet pickle relish
1 tablespoon balsamic vinegar

In a large bowl combine all of the ingredients and refrigerate for about 2 to 3 hours to allow flavors to develop before serving. *Serves 4.*

Nutritional information per serving:

calories = 220	carbohydrate = 41g	cholesterol = 0mg
sodium = 335mg	protein = 13g	fat = 1g
calories from fat = 7		

Black-Eyed Pea Salad

This recipe is an interpretation of a dish I sampled while dining aboard a cruise ship on the Nile in Egypt.

2 cups cooked black-eyed peas
½ cup diced tomatoes
½ cup diced red onions
½ cup diced carrots
1 teaspoon olive oil

1 tablespoon balsamic vinegar
1 teaspoon freshly ground black
  pepper
½ teaspoon ground cumin

In a large bowl, careful not to crush the peas, stir together the peas, tomatoes, onions, and carrots. In a cup combine the olive oil, vinegar, pepper, and cumin. Pour over the vegetables. Chill the salad in the refrigerator for at least 2 hours for the flavors to blend. *Serves 4.*

Nutritional information per serving:

calories = 140   carbohydrate = 24g   cholesterol = 0mg
sodium = 20mg   protein = 8g   fat = 2g
calories from fat = 19

Fresh Beet Salad

Besides beets, other root vegetables such as turnips and radishes can be added to this salad.

*2 pounds fresh beets, stems trimmed
   to about 2 inches
½ cup chopped red onion
½ cup sliced white mushrooms
1 tablespoon cider vinegar*

*1 teaspoon chopped fresh parsley
½ teaspoon Soul Food Seasoning
   (see page 123)
½ teaspoon freshly ground black
   pepper*

In a large pot, boil the beets in about 2 quarts of water (or enough to cover the beets) for about 20 minutes or until they are slightly tender (do not overcook, because the texture will become too soft). Remove the beets from the water and let them cool. Peel the beets with a sharp paring knife, cut them up into bite-size cubes (about 1/4 inch), and place them in a large bowl. Add the onion, mushrooms, vinegar, parsley, Soul Food Seasoning, and pepper and mix well. Refrigerate 2 to 3 hours, to allow flavors to develop, before serving. *Serves 6.*

Nutritional information per serving:

calories = 75
sodium = 110mg
calories from fat = 2

carbohydrate = 17g
protein = 3g

cholesterol = 0mg
fat = <1g

Carrot Salad

Adding a few sliced, toasted almonds gives this recipe a delicious flavor, as well as a distinguished appearance.

1 pound carrots, shredded
½ cup nonfat mayonnaise
½ cup dark raisins
½ cup golden raisins
1 tablespoon cider vinegar
1 tablespoon sugar

In a large bowl, combine all the ingredients and mix well. For a creamier texture, use more nonfat mayonnaise. Chill in the refrigerator for 2 hours before serving. *Serves 6.*

Nutritional information per serving:

calories = 130	carbohydrate = 33g	cholesterol = 0mg
sodium = 196mg	protein = 2g	fat = <1g
calories from fat = 2		

Classic Potato Salad

A bowl of potato salad is traditionally on the menu for special summer meals. This recipe can be prepared in larger quantities by doubling or tripling the ingredients.

3 cups of white potatoes, peeled, cooked, and cut into 1-inch cubes
½ cup chopped celery
¼ cup sweet pickle relish
¼ cup sliced scallions (green onions)

1 tablespoon balsamic vinegar
1 tablespoon finely chopped fresh dill
1 ½ teaspoons Dijon mustard
½ teaspoon ground white pepper

In a large bowl, combine all the ingredients, mixing well. Chill in the refrigerator for at least 2 hours, to allow flavors to develop, before serving. *Serves 4.*

Nutritional information per serving:
calories = 180
sodium = 199mg
calories from fat = 4

carbohydrate = 43g
protein = 4g

cholesterol = 0mg
fat = <1g

Cole Slaw

This cole slaw gets its bright citrus flavor from the lemon juice and zest. Regular white distilled vinegar (which is a common ingredient in cole slaw) delivers a less zesty flavor, but can be used instead of lemon.

2 cups shredded green cabbage
2 cups shredded red cabbage
½ cup shredded carrots
¼ cup diced onion
¼ cup diced sweet pickles
3 tablespoons nonfat plain yogurt

2 tablespoons sugar
2 tablespoons freshly squeezed
  lemon juice
½ teaspoon lemon zest (grated from
  the lemon peel)

Mix all the ingredients thoroughly in a large bowl. Chill in the refrigerator for 2 to 3 hours before serving. *Serves 4*

Nutritional information per serving:

calories = 80	carbohydrate = 20g	cholesterol = 0mg
sodium = 149mg	protein = 2g	fat = <1g
calories from fat = 2		

Cucumber Salad

I think this seasonal summer salad is even more enjoyable when cilantro (also known as Chinese parsley and fresh coriander) is used instead of Italian parsley, but follow your own taste when deciding which to use.

2 ½ cups thinly sliced unpeeled
   cucumbers
¼ cup cubed tomatoes
1 tablespoon chopped fresh Italian
   parsley

1 teaspoon chopped fresh tarragon
¼ cup diced onion
2 tablespoons balsamic vinegar
1 teaspoon freshly ground black
   pepper

Combine the cucumbers, tomatoes, parsley, tarragon, and onion in a large bowl. In a cup, combine the vinegar and pepper and pour over the salad. Mix well and chill in the refrigerator for about 3 hours, to allow flavors to develop, before serving. *Serves 4.*

Nutritional information per serving:

calories = 25
sodium = 5mg
calories from fat = 2

carbohydrate = 5g
protein = 1g

cholesterol = 0mg
fat = <1g

ONION Salad

Vidalia onions, which are known as the world's sweetest, can be used as an alternative to the ones suggested in this recipe.

1 cup sliced scallions
1 cup sliced Spanish onion
1 cup sliced white onion
¼ cup low-fat mozzarella cheese,
  shredded
2 slices toasted whole wheat bread,
  cut into ½-inch cubes (optional)

3 tablespoons cider vinegar
1 teaspoon freshly ground black
  pepper

Mix all the ingredients together in a large bowl and chill in the refrigerator 3 hours, to allow flavors to develop, before serving. *Serves 4 to 6.*

Nutritional information per serving:

calories = 100	carbohydrate = 11g	cholesterol = 0mg
sodium = 321mg	protein = 15g	fat = <1g
calories from fat = 4		

Macaroni Salad

This recipe calls for dill pickles, but sweet pickles can be used if you prefer.

3 cups cooked elbow macaroni
¼ cup diced celery
¼ cup diced dill pickle
3 tablespoons diced pimiento

2 tablespoons diced onion
3 tablespoons nonfat plain yogurt
1 teaspoon chopped fresh dill
½ teaspoon ground red pepper

In a large bowl, mix the pasta, celery, pickle, pimiento, and onion. In a separate bowl, blend together the yogurt, dill, and pepper. Add the dressing to the pasta and mix thoroughly. Chill in the refrigerator for about 3 hours, to allow flavors to develop, before serving. *Serves 4.*

Nutritional information per serving:

calories = 150	carbohydrate = 30g	cholesterol = 0mg
sodium = 77mg	protein = 5g	fat = 1g
calories from fat = 7		

String Bean Salad

A nonfat Italian dressing can be used in this bean salad instead of balsamic vinegar if you prefer a sweeter, smoother flavor.

*1 pound fresh string beans, steamed
    to desired tenderness*
½ cup diced tomato
½ cup diced cucumber

¼ cup diced green bell peppers
¼ cup diced onion
3 tablespoons Dijon mustard
1 tablespoon balsamic vinegar

In a large bowl, combine the string beans, tomato, cucumber, bell pepper, and onion. In a cup combine the mustard and vinegar. Pour the dressing over the vegetables and mix well. Chill in the refrigerator for 1 to 2 hours, to allow flavors to develop, before serving. *Serves 6.*

Nutritional information per serving:

calories = 45
sodium = 124mg
calories from fat = 6

carbohydrate = 9g
protein = 2g

cholesterol = 0mg
fat = 1g

Country-Style Chicken Salad

This chicken salad can be served cold on a bed of lettuce with fresh vegetables such as carrots, zucchini, and broccoli or eaten in a sandwich. It can also be slightly warmed.

3 cups cubed poached boneless, skinless chicken breast
½ cup diced onion
½ cup diced celery
¼ cup cubed sweet pickles

⅓ cup nonfat plain yogurt
1 teaspoon curry powder
1 teaspoon freshly ground black pepper

In a bowl, combine the chicken, onion, celery, and pickles. In another bowl, stir the yogurt, curry powder, and pepper together. Pour the dressing over the chicken and blend well. Chill the salad in the refrigerator for about 1 hour, to allow flavors to develop, before serving. *Serves 4.*

Nutritional information per serving:

calories = 175	carbohydrate = 10g	cholesterol = 81mg
sodium = 195mg	protein = 27g	fat = 3g
calories from fat = 25		

Forgotten Pork Salad

This traditional recipe calls for "leftover" oven-baked pork roast or barbecue pork roast. Remember to separate and discard all the fat from the meat.

2 cups chopped romaine lettuce
½ cup chopped cooked lean pork roast
½ cup diced scallions (green part only)

½ cup shredded red cabbage
½ cup shredded carrots
2 tablespoons cider vinegar
1 teaspoon freshly ground black pepper

Mix all the ingredients in a large bowl. Let chill in the refrigerator for at least 1 hour, to allow flavors to develop, before serving. *Serves 4.*

Nutritional information per serving:

calories = 80
sodium = 26mg
calories from fat = 31

carbohydrate = 3g
protein = 9g

cholesterol = 17mg
fat = 3g

Turkey Ham Salad

Smoked skinless turkey breast or poached skinless chicken breast can be used as a substitute for the smoked turkey ham in this recipe.

1 ½ cups peeled and diced cucumbers
1 cup diced white mushrooms
½ cup diced green bell pepper
½ cup diced red bell pepper
¼ cup diced lean smoked turkey ham

¼ cup nonfat mayonnaise
3 tablespoons diced sweet pickles
2 tablespoons diced onion
1 teaspoon freshly ground black pepper

Mix all the ingredients together and chill in the refrigerator at least 1 hour, to allow flavors to develop, before serving. *Serves 6.*

Nutritional information per serving:

calories = 50	carbohydrate = 8g	cholesterol = 6mg
sodium = 259mg	protein = 2g	fat = 1g
calories from fat = 6		

Turkey Salad

This recipe calls for poached skinless, boneless turkey breast. If you have leftovers from a roasted turkey, it makes a great turkey salad, but remember to trim the fat and remove the skin.

2 cups poached skinless, boneless
    turkey breast
½ cup diced celery
¼ cup nonfat plain yogurt

¼ cup diced green bell pepper
¼ cup diced red bell pepper
1 teaspoon chopped fresh dill
½ teaspoon white pepper

Mix all the ingredients together in a large bowl. Chill in the refrigerator for 3 to 4 hours, to allow flavors to develop, before serving. *Serves 4.*

Nutritional information per serving:

calories = 170	carbohydrate = 3g	cholesterol = 95mg
sodium = 83mg	protein = 35g	fat = 1g
calories from fat = 8		

Dandelion Salad

This salad recipe calls for young dandelion leaves because the texture is tender. Older (bigger) dandelion leaves are usually tough and have to be cooked first.

1 pound young dandelion leaves
2 slices turkey bacon
1 ½ tablespoons balsamic vinegar

½ teaspoon freshly ground black
pepper

Wash and dry the dandelion leaves and place in a serving dish. To make the dressing, put the 2 slices of turkey bacon into a skillet and cook over medium heat for about 2 minutes on each side. Remove the bacon from the skillet and place on paper towels to let the fat drain. Cut both cooked slices into 1/2-inch pieces. Place the bacon in the serving dish with the dandelion leaves. Drizzle the balsamic vinegar on top along with the pepper. Toss the salad slightly and serve. *Serves 4.*

Nutritional information per serving:

calories = 75
sodium = 191mg
calories from fat = 21

carbohydrate = 21g
protein = 5g

cholesterol = 5mg
fat = 2g

Bean Cucumber and Tomato Salad

Cooked kidney beans or black beans can be used as a substitute for the cannelloni beans in this recipe. They are equally delicious and nutritious.

3 cups cooked white beans (such as
  navy or cannelloni beans)
1 cup peeled and seeded diced
  cucumber
¼ cup seeded diced tomato

1 teaspoon freshly chopped dill
1 teaspoon freshly chopped tarragon
1 tablespoon nonfat mayonnaise
1 tablespoon dijon mustard

In a large bowl combine the beans, cucumber, and tomato. In a cup combine the dill, tarragon, mayonnaise, and mustard. Pour the mustard dressing over the vegetables and mix well. Chill in the refrigerator for 1 to 2 hours (to allow flavors to develop) before serving. Serves 4.

Nutritional information per serving:
calories = 202   carbohydrate = 36g   cholesterol = 0mg
sodium = 167mg   protein = 14g   fat = 1g
calories from fat = 8

Main Dishes

Red Beans and Rice

This healthy version of red beans and rice rivals the traditional version which is made with smoked ham hocks and pork sausage.

2 cups dried kidney beans
1 pound skinless smoked turkey breast, cut up in cubes
1 cup chopped onion
1 tablespoon minced fresh garlic

1 tablespoon Soul Food Seasoning (see page 123)
1 teaspoon celery seeds
1 bay leaf
2 cups long-grain white rice

Sort and rinse the beans. Place the beans in a pot with the turkey breast, and add enough water to cover completely. Bring to a boil, then reduce the heat to low; cover and simmer for about 2 hours. Add the onion, garlic, Soul Food Seasoning, celery seeds, and bay leaf and cook for an additional 45 minutes. In a separate pot, bring 5 cups of water to a boil. Add the rice, cover, reduce heat, and simmer for about 20 minutes. Serve the beans over the rice or combine rice and beans together in a large serving bowl. *Serves 8.*

Nutritional information per serving:

calories = 260
sodium = 38mg
calories from fat = 10

carbohydrate = 35g
protein = 26mg

cholesterol = 47mg
fat = 1g

Baked Lima Beans

Baked lima beans are a rich source of protein. They can be served as a stew over rice or eaten with Jalapeño Corn Bread (see page 17).

3 cups dried lima beans
⅓ pound skinless smoked turkey
    breast
1 cup nonfat canned chicken broth
½ cup diced onions
⅓ cup diced carrots

1 tablespoon minced fresh garlic
1 tablespoon Soul Food Seasoning
    (see page 123)
1 teaspoon freshly ground black
    pepper
1 bay leaf

Place the lima beans in a Dutch oven or large pot, and cover them with water. Let them soak for 3 hours at room temperature. Drain the water, sort the beans, rinse them thoroughly, and place them back in the Dutch oven. Preheat oven to 350°F. Add the turkey, chicken stock, onion, carrots, garlic, Soul Food Seasoning, pepper, and bay leaf to the beans. Add enough water to cover the beans by about 2 inches. Cover and bake for about 2 to 3 hours. Make sure water is on top of the beans throughout the cooking time; if not, add more water. When done, the beans should be tender—do not overcook. *Serves 10.*

Nutritional information per serving:

calories = 90	carbohydrate = 15g	cholesterol = 11mg
sodium = 47mg	protein = 8g	fat = <1g
calories from fat = 3		

Red Beans
and Tomato Sauce

Red beans and tomato sauce can be served over rice or cooked pasta.

2 ½ cups dried kidney beans
½ cup chopped carrot
1 cup chopped onion
1 8-ounce can tomato sauce

2 teaspoons celery seeds
1 teaspoon minced fresh garlic
1 bay leaf

Sort and rinse the beans and place them in a pot with the carrot and onion. Completely cover with water. Simmer, covered, for 1 1/2 hours over a medium heat or until tender. Transfer the beans (discarding any excess liquid if desired) to a large skillet, and add the tomato sauce, celery seeds, garlic, and bay leaf, and cook for about 45 minutes more on a low heat, stirring occasionally. *Serves 6 to 8.*

Nutritional information per serving:

calories = 170
sodium = 182mg
calories from fat = 8

carbohydrate = 31g
protein = 10g

cholesterol = 0mg
fat = 1g

Black-Eyed Peas

In this recipe, smoked turkey makes a great, healthful alternative to the smoked pork traditionally used in cooking black-eyed peas. Served over Skillet Corn Bread (see page 20).

3 cups dried black-eyed peas
1 cup chopped skinless smoked
* turkey breast*
1 cup chopped onion
½ cup chopped carrot
½ cup chopped celery

2 tablespoons cider vinegar
2 tablespoons Soul Food Seasoning
* (see page 123)*
1 teaspoon fresh ground black
* pepper*

Rinse and sort the peas. Place them in a large pot with enough water to cover and bring to boil. Once boiling, remove the pot from the heat, cover, and let stand for 1 1/2 hours. Add the remaining ingredients and additional water if necessary to cover the peas. Place a lid on the pot, and cook on a low-medium heat for about 1 hour, or until the peas are tender. Make sure there is enough water added in the pot to cover the peas throughout the cooking time. *Serves 8 to 10.*

Nutritional information per serving:

calories = 95	carbohydrate = 14g	cholesterol = 19mg
sodium = 28mg	protein = 9g	fat = <1g
calories from fat = 4		

Collard Greens

Cooking collard greens the traditional way usually requires some type of smoked pork to be used as a flavor enhancer. Using smoked turkey bacon, however, gives a similar flavor and makes for a healthier, lower-fat dish.

3 pounds collard greens, rinsed and chopped
½ pound smoked turkey breast, cubed
1 cup nonfat chicken broth

½ cup minced onion
1 teaspoon crushed red pepper flakes
1 teaspoon minced celery
1 teaspoon freshly ground black pepper

Place the collard greens and turkey in a large pot. Cover them with water, and cook on a medium heat, covered, for 20 minutes. Add the chicken broth, onion, red pepper flakes, celery, and black pepper, and cook on a low-medium heat, covered, for about 45 minutes. *Serves 8.*

Nutritional information per serving:

calories = 95	carbohydrate = 13g	cholesterol = 24mg
sodium = 78mg	protein = 11g	fat = 1g
calories from fat = 6		

Fried Yellow Squash with Zucchini

Vegetables such as broccoli, cauliflower, and Portobello mushrooms can be used as alternatives in this recipe.

nonstick cooking spray
1 pound yellow squash, sliced ½-inch thick
1 pound zucchini, sliced ½-inch thick
1 cup chopped onion
1 cup chopped white mushrooms

½ pound smoked skinless turkey breast, chopped
1 teaspoon chopped fresh parsley
1 teaspoon Soul Food Seasoning (see page 123)
1 teaspoon freshly ground black pepper

Heat a large nonstick frying pan sprayed with cooking spray and cook the yellow squash, zucchini, onion, and mushrooms over low heat, covered, for about 15 minutes. Add the turkey, parsley, Soul Food Seasoning, and black pepper, and continue to cook for about 30 minutes or until the vegetables are tender. Keep covered so that the juices from the vegetables do not evaporate. *Serves 6.*

Nutritional information per serving:
calories = 110
sodium = 35mg
calories from fat = 9

carbohydrate = 9g
protein = 18g

cholesterol = 43mg
fat = 1g

Mixed Greens

For a long time, mixed greens have been a favorite in African-American families. When greens are cooked the traditional way they usually consist of some type of smoked pork, which makes the greens high in fat and cholesterol. However, if greens are cooked with a healthier meat such as skinless smoked turkey or skinless smoked chicken, it becomes a very healthy dish.

1 pound mustard greens
1 pound turnip greens
1 pound spinach
½ cup chopped fresh turnips
1 cup chopped smoked skinless
  chicken breast

1 teaspoon white vinegar
1 tablespoon Soul Food Seasoning
  (see page 123)
1 teaspoon crushed red pepper flakes
  (optional)
1 teaspoon celery seeds

Clean and rinse the mustard and turnip greens (removing the stems) in cold water. Drain and set aside. Rinse the spinach in cold water (but do not remove the stems). Place the greens, spinach, turnips, chicken, vinegar, Soul Food Seasoning, red pepper flakes, and celery seeds in a large pot, and cover with water. Cook for about 1 hour on a medium heat or until tender. *Serves 8.*

Nutritional information per serving:

calories = 100	carbohydrate = 11g	cholesterol = 24mg
sodium = 104mg	protein = 12g	fat = 1g
calories from fat = 13		

Black-Eyed Pea Soulburger

This recipe is a vegetarian delight and can be eaten with or without a hamburger bun. Top with sweet relish or Citrus or Herbal Barbecue Sauce (see pages 121 and 122).

2 cups black-eyed peas, cooked and drained
½ cup cooked, cubed cauliflower florets
½ cup cooked, cubed broccoli stems
½ cup fresh white mushrooms, chopped
2 teaspoons all-purpose flour

3 egg whites, lightly beaten
2 teaspoons Soul Food Seasoning (see page 123)
1 teaspoon minced fresh garlic
1 teaspoon horseradish
1 teaspoon Worcestershire sauce
nonstick cooking spray

Preheat oven to 400°F. In a large bowl, mix all the ingredients together thoroughly, lightly mashing the peas against the sides of the bowl. Pat the ingredients into 3-inch to 4-inch burgers and place on a baking pan lightly coated with nonstick cooking spray. Lightly coat each burger with cooking spray so that they can be flipped easily and bake for 10 minutes or until the burgers are firm on one side, then flip and cook another 10 minutes. *Serves 4.*

Nutritional information per burger:

calories = 120	carbohydrate = 19g	cholesterol = 0mg
sodium = 82mg	protein = 10g	fat = 1g
calories from fat = 9		

Unfried Chicken

The oil used to make traditional fried chicken — not to mention the skin that is usually left on the meat — turns the old favorite into a high-fat no-no. This unfried "fried" chicken is just as crunchy and tasty as the "real thing," but it hasn't got the fat from the skin and the oil.

3 tablespoons fresh lime juice
1 cup skim milk
4 ice cubes
1 ½ pounds of boneless, skinless
  chicken breast
nonstick cooking spray
½ cup unbleached flour

2 teaspoons paprika
1 teaspoon celery seeds
2 tablespoons Soul Food Seasoning
  (see page 123)
2 teaspoons freshly ground black
  pepper

In a large bowl, combine the lime juice, milk, and ice cubes. Add the chicken breasts and refrigerate for about 2 hours. Preheat oven to 375°F. Lightly coat a baking pan with nonstick cooking spray. In a large resealable plastic bag, combine the flour, paprika, celery seeds, Soul Food Seasoning, and black pepper. Put the chicken breasts, one at a time, in the plastic bag and shake well. Place each chicken breast on the baking pan. Spray each chicken piece with some cooking spray. Bake for about an hour. Turn the chicken over every 15 minutes to assure even crispiness. *Serves 4 to 6.*

Nutritional information per serving:

calories = 200	carbohydrate = 14g	cholesterol = 82mg
sodium = 64mg	protein = 28g	fat = 3g
calories from fat = 27		

Hot Spaghetti with Ground Turkey

This recipe is dedicated to my grandfather, Frank Randle, a man who could make the hottest spaghetti!

nonstick cooking spray
1 pound ground fresh skinless
    turkey breast
1 tablespoon crushed red pepper
    flakes (optional)
2 teaspoons freshly ground black
    pepper
1 teaspoon Soul Food Seasoning
    (see page 123)

1 teaspoon minced fresh garlic
½ teaspoon fresh rosemary
1 crushed bay leaf
1 8-ounce can tomato sauce
1 pound spaghetti, cooked and
    drained

In a large nonstick frying pan lightly coated with cooking spray, sauté the ground turkey, red pepper flakes, black pepper, Soul Food Seasoning, garlic, rosemary, and bay leaf. Cook over a medium heat for about 10 minutes or until turkey is no longer pink, stirring frequently. Add the tomato sauce and continue to cook for another 10 minutes. Place the cooked spaghetti in a large pasta bowl and toss with the tomato sauce. *Serves 4 to 6.*

Nutritional information per serving:

calories = 330	carbohydrate = 40g	cholesterol = 71mg
sodium = 92mg	protein = 34g	fat = 4g
calories from fat = 38		

Pinto Beans and Smoked Turkey

Cooking pinto beans with smoked turkey instead of ham hocks keeps out much of the unnecessary fat and cholesterol.

3 cups dried pinto beans
1 ½ pounds smoked skinless turkey breasts, cubed
1 tablespoon Soul Food Seasoning (see page 123)

2 tablespoons cider vinegar
2 bay leaves

Soak the beans in enough water to cover for 4 hours, or overnight. After soaking, sort and rinse the beans and place them in a large pot with the turkey breasts, Soul Food Seasoning, vinegar, and bay leaves. Add water until the breasts and beans are covered. Cook over a low-medium heat, covered, for about 2 1/2 hours or until the beans are tender but not overcooked. *Serves 10.*

Nutritional information per serving:

calories = 280
sodium = 40mg
calories from fat = 11

carbohydrate = 36g
protein = 32g

cholesterol = 57mg
fat = 1g

Salmon Patties

Crab meat can be used in this recipe instead of salmon.

1 pound fresh salmon, bones and
    skin removed
2 cups cooked white potatoes, cut up
    into small cubes
2 teaspoons sliced scallions, green
    part only
1 tablespoon fresh lemon juice

2 teaspoons paprika
1 teaspoon crushed fennel seeds
1 teaspoon ground white pepper
2 egg whites, lightly beaten
½ cup cubed toasted whole wheat
    bread
nonstick cooking spray

Grind salmon in a food processor or mince finely. Mix all the ingredients well. Pat the mixture into 3-inch patties and cook for about 5 minutes on each side over medium heat in a nonstick frying pan sprayed with cooking spray. Make sure that the patties are brown and firm on each side before removing them from the frying pan. *Serves 6.*

Nutritional information per patty:

calories = 170
sodium = 104mg
calories from fat = 43

carbohydrate = 22g
protein = 11g

cholesterol = 22mg
fat = 5g

Smothered Cabbage
with Smoked Turkey

If you are not fond of cabbage, try fresh collard greens in this recipe instead. However, collard greens require about 15 to 20 minutes of cooking time.

5 cups chopped cabbage
1 cup smoked skinless turkey
   breast, chopped
½ cup sliced carrot

1 tablespoon balsamic vinegar
1 tablespoon sugar
1 teaspoon ground white pepper

Pour 2 cups of water in a large skillet and bring to a boil. Add the cabbage, turkey, carrots, vinegar, sugar, and pepper. Cover the pan and cook for about 1 hour over a low-medium heat, stirring occasionally. Do not let all of the water evaporate from the pan; add more if needed so that the cabbage does not burn. *Serves 6.*

Nutritional information per serving:
calories = 75
sodium = 34mg
calories from fat = 4

carbohydrate = 6g
protein = 12g

cholesterol = 32mg
fat = <1g

Smothered Chicken

This recipe can be served with Cream-Like Potatoes (see page 79).

nonstick cooking spray
3 tablespoons flour
½ cup chopped onion
1 tablespoon chopped fresh garlic
½ teaspoon celery seeds
1 tablespoon Soul Food Seasoning
   (see page 123)

1 teaspoon freshly ground black
   pepper
1 ½ pounds skinless, boneless
   chicken breasts

Thoroughly mix the flour with about four tablespoons of water to make a thin sauce. In a nonstick skillet coated with nonstick cooking spray, heat the flour mixture over medium-low heat, stirring continuously for about 10 minutes or until a smooth sauce is formed (add more water if necessary). Stir in the onion, garlic, celery seeds, Soul Food Seasoning, black pepper, and two cups of water. Add the chicken. Cover and simmer for about 45 minutes, or until the chicken is cooked all the way through. *Serves 6.*

Nutritional information per serving:

calories = 160	carbohydrate = 7g	cholesterol = 81mg
sodium = 40mg	protein = 26g	fat = 3g
calories from fat = 25		

Spinach, Chicken, and Rice

This is a one-dish meal for which the requirements are only hungry people.

nonstick cooking spray
2 pounds boneless, skinless chicken
  breast, cut into 1-inch cubes
1 pound fresh spinach, rinsed and
  chopped
2 cups long-grain white rice

1 bay leaf
1 teaspoon fresh rosemary
2 teaspoons fresh dill
2 tablespoons fresh lemon juice
1 teaspoon freshly ground black
  pepper

In a nonstick skillet lightly coated with nonstick cooking spray, sauté the chicken for about 10 minutes on medium heat or until lightly browned. Add the spinach and sauté until it is completely wilted, stirring continuously. Add the rice, the remaining ingredients, and 4 cups of water. Cover and cook over low heat for about 20 minutes. *Serves 6.*

Nutritional information per serving:

calories = 180	carbohydrate = 19g	cholesterol = 54mg
sodium = 77mg	protein = 21g	fat = 2g
calories from fat = 19		

Stuffed Pork Tenderloin with Vegetables

Fresh vegetables as a stuffing for pork tenderloin instead of fatty, greasy bread stuffing not only taste fresher, but they can also count as a serving of vegetables.

½ cup diced broccoli stems
½ cup diced cauliflower florets
¼ cup diced carrots
1 egg white, lightly beaten
1 tablespoon fresh lime juice, plus 1 teaspoon
½ teaspoon dried rubbed sage

2 lean pork tenderloins (about 2 pounds)
2 tablespoons minced fresh garlic
1 teaspoon freshly ground black pepper
nonstick cooking spray

Preheat oven to 400°F. In a bowl, mix the broccoli, cauliflower, carrots, egg white, lime juice, and sage. Set aside. Along the length of each tenderloin, slice a pocket deep enough for half of the stuffing. Stuff each tenderloin with the stuffing, season them with garlic and pepper, and place them in a roasting pan lightly coated with cooking spray. Sprinkle some additional lime juice on top of the tenderloins and spray each with cooking spray. Cover the pan tightly with foil and roast for about 1 hour turning the tenderloins halfway through cooking. *Serves 4 to 6.*

Nutritional information per serving:

calories = 215	carbohydrate = 3g	cholesterol = 80mg
sodium = 121mg	protein = 35g	fat = 6g
calories from fat = 56		

Kale with Smoked Turkey

This recipe calls for cider vinegar but other flavored vinegars such as garlic, raspberry, and malt can be used.

2 pounds kale
1 cup chopped onion
½ pound smoked turkey breast

½ teaspoon red pepper flakes
2 tablespoons cider vinegar

Wash the kale thoroughly under cool running water, then shake off excess water and pinch the leaves off the stems. Place the leaves, onion, turkey breast, and pepper in a large heavy skillet. Cover and cook over medium heat for 20 minutes or until the kale is tender. Add the vinegar and transfer to a warm serving dish. *Makes 6 servings.*

Nutritional information per serving:

calories = 63	carbohydrate = 5g	cholesterol = 13mg
sodium = 338mg	protein = 9g	fat = 1g
calories from fat = 13		

Pork and Beans

Smoked turkey breast can be used as a substitute for the pork in this recipe.

2 ½ cups dried navy beans
¼ cup dark molasses
1 teaspoon worcestershire sauce
2 teaspoons dry mustard
1 tablespoon light brown sugar

½ teaspoon freshly ground black
   pepper
¼ pound lean pork lion, cut into
   chunks
1 ½ cups diced onion

Place the navy beans in a bowl and cover them with water. Let them soak for at least 4 hours, preferably overnight. Strain the beans, reserving the water in a skillet. Put the beans in a baking casserole dish and set aside.

Preheat the oven to 350°F. Heat the bean water over medium heat for 1 minute and stir in the molasses, worcestershire sauce, mustard, sugar, and black pepper. Stir for two minutes. Add the green pepper, pork, and onion and stir for one minute.

Pour the bean water mixture over the top of the beans. Cover and bake for about 1 hour or until the beans are soft. During the cooking stage, if the beans seem to be getting dry, add more water. *Serves 6 to 8.*

Nutritional information per serving:

calories = 152
sodium = 29mg
calories from fat = 17

carbohydrate = 25g
protein = 10g

cholesterol = 9mg
fat = 2g

Side Dishes

Mississippi Dirty Rice

When I was a child, I was told that many moons ago, the dirt from the hills of Mississippi was so sweet and tasty that local people used it to thicken gravies, add flavor to baked goods, and make dirty rice.

1 cup brown rice
½ cup ground all-white turkey
¼ cup diced onion
2 tablespoons diced green bell pepper
1 tablespoon Soul Food Seasoning
  (see page 123)

1 teaspoon chopped fresh garlic
1 teaspoon freshly ground black
  pepper
nonstick cooking spray

Bring 3 cups of water to a boil in a medium saucepan and add the rice. Cover and cook for about 50 minutes over a low-medium heat; set aside. Sauté the ground turkey, onion, green pepper, Soul Food Seasoning, garlic, and black pepper in a nonstick skillet lightly coated with nonstick cooking spray for about 15 minutes over a low heat. In a large bowl, stir together the rice and turkey mixture. *Serves 4.*

Nutritional information per serving:

calories = 160	carbohydrate = 26g	cholesterol = 18mg
sodium = 26mg	protein = 9g	fat = 2g
calories from fat = 17		

Corn Pudding

If fresh corn is not available, substitute thawed frozen corn.

nonstick cooking spray
4 cups fresh uncooked corn, cut off
   the cob
3 tablespoons red bell pepper, diced

1 cup skim milk
2 egg whites, lightly beaten
1 teaspoon fresh lemon juice
1 teaspoon celery seeds

Preheat oven to 350°F. Lightly coat a 6-cup casserole with cooking spray and set aside. Mix all the ingredients well in a large bowl. Add more milk if a more pudding-like texture is desired. Pour the ingredients into the casserole, cover, and bake about 45 minutes, or until the texture of the pudding is solid and firm. *Serves 4.*

Nutritional information per serving:

calories = 280
sodium = 99mg
calories from fat = 29

carbohydrate = 61g
protein = 11g

cholesterol = 1mg
fat = 3g

Cream-Like Potatoes

For a more exotic flavor, add a tablespoon of horseradish to this recipe.

2 pounds white potatoes
¾ cup plain nonfat yogurt
¼ cup skim milk
2 tablespoons Dijon mustard

1 teaspoon ground white pepper
1 teaspoon fresh lemon juice
1 tablespoon nonfat Parmesan
  cheese topping

Peel the potatoes and cut them into quarters. Rinse well. Cook them in boiling water for about 20 minutes or until fork-tender. Drain the potatoes and place in a large bowl. Add the yogurt, milk, Dijon, pepper, and lemon juice. Mash well with a potato masher, leaving no lumps. For a drier or creamier texture, adjust the amount of milk. Sprinkle the Parmesan cheese on top of the potatoes and serve. *Serves 4.*

Nutritional information per serving:

calories = 245	carbohydrate = 52g	cholesterol = 1mg
sodium = 250mg	protein = 8g	fat = 1g
calories from fat = 7		

Scalloped Potatoes

You can substitute sweet potatoes for white potatoes in this recipe. If you do, use nutmeg, cardamom, and ginger instead of scallions, mushrooms, and dill.

1 cup skim milk
3 cups peeled white potatoes, thinly sliced
½ cup sliced white button mushrooms
2 tablespoons finely chopped fresh parsley

2 tablespoons finely chopped onion
2 tablespoons finely chopped scallions
1 tablespoon fresh lemon juice
1 teaspoon ground white pepper

Heat the skim milk in a large skillet for about 3 minutes. Add the potatoes and mushrooms, and cook on a low heat for 20 minutes or until the texture becomes soft. Stir constantly to avoid sticking or burning, but be careful not to break potato slices. Add the parsley, onions, scallions, lemon juice, and white pepper. Cook another 5 minutes, stirring frequently. *Serves 6.*

Nutritional information per serving:

calories = 70	carbohydrate = 15g	cholesterol = 1mg
sodium = 25mg	protein = 3g	fat = <1g
calories from fat = 2		

Twice-Baked Potatoes with Turkey Bacon

Additional horseradish or Dijon mustard can be added for a tangier flavor.

6 large baked Idaho potatoes (about 4 pounds)
¼ cup skim milk
2 tablespoons diced onion
1 tablespoon chopped fresh cilantro
1 tablespoon paprika, plus more for garnish

1 tablespoon freshly ground black pepper
1 teaspoon prepared horseradish
1 egg white, lightly beaten
¼ cup cooked and crumbled crisp turkey bacon

Preheat oven to 400°F. Cut the potatoes lengthwise in half. Scoop out the pulp, being careful to save the skins so that they are like empty boats. Place the pulp in a bowl and mash with skim milk, onion, cilantro, paprika, black pepper, horseradish, and egg white. Mix the pulp well so that no lumps remain. Blend in the turkey bacon. Fill the potato shells with the mixture. Sprinkle some additional paprika on top. Bake about 25 minutes or until slightly browned and stiff. *Serves 12.*

Nutritional information per serving:
calories = 100
carbohydrate = 18g
cholesterol = 5mg
sodium = 125mg
protein = 4g
fat = 2g
calories from fat = 16

Fried Turkey and Rice

Broccoli and yellow or green bell peppers can be used as alternative ingredients in this recipe.

¼ cup diced carrot

¼ cup diced onion

3 tablespoons diced scallions

¼ cup diced red bell pepper

2 tablespoons low-sodium soy sauce

nonstick cooking spray

2 ½ cups cooked long-grain white rice

½ cup chopped skinless cooked turkey breast

2 egg whites

Sauté the carrot, onion, scallions, red pepper, and soy sauce for about 10 minutes on a medium heat in a large frying pan lightly coated with cooking spray. Add the rice, turkey, and egg whites to the pan and cook, stirring constantly, for 2 minutes or until the eggs have cooked thoroughly. *Serves 4.*

Nutritional information per serving:

calories = 170

sodium = 262mg

calories from fat = 10

carbohydrate = 31g

protein = 7g

cholesterol = 6mg

fat = 1g

Fresh Fried Corn

Fresh corn must be used in this recipe. Neither frozen nor canned corn will deliver the best results.

3 cups fresh corn cut from the cob
¼ cup diced green bell pepper
2 tablespoons skim milk
1 tablespoon all-purpose flour

1 teaspoon minced fresh garlic
1 teaspoon ground white pepper
½ teaspoon paprika
nonstick cooking spray

Combine the corn, green pepper, milk, flour, garlic, white pepper, and paprika in a large nonstick skillet lightly coated with cooking spray. Cook for about 20 minutes over low-medium heat, stirring constantly, to avoid sticking. *Serves 4.*

Nutritional information per serving:

calories = 120
sodium = 11mg
calories from fat = 4

carbohydrate = 29g
protein = 4g

cholesterol = 0mg
fat = <1g

HoMeMade Fries

These oven-baked fries can be served with the Citrus or Herbal Barbecue Sauce for dipping (see pages 121 and 122).

nonstick cooking spray
2 pounds Idaho potatoes
3 egg whites, lightly beaten
½ cup all-purpose flour

1 tablespoon Soul Food Seasoning
  (see page 123)
½ teaspoon crushed celery seeds

Preheat oven to 400°F. Lightly coat a baking sheet with cooking spray. Peel the potatoes, cut them lengthwise into about 1/4-inch-thick sticks, and place them in a large bowl. Pour the egg whites over them and toss to coat all the potato slices. Combine the flour, Soul Food Seasoning, and celery seeds in a plastic bag. Remove about one handful of potatoes from the bowl and drain off any excess egg white. Put the potatoes in the bag and shake well to coat the potatoes. Remove the potatoes from the bag and spread them on the baking sheet. Repeat until all the potatoes are coated. Spray the potatoes with cooking spray. Bake for 30 minutes or until the fries are crispy, turning them every 10 minutes with a spatula, so that they are brown and crispy all over. *Serves 4.*

Nutritional information per serving:

calories = 145	carbohydrate = 29g	cholesterol = 0mg
sodium = 55mg	protein = 6g	fat = <1g
calories from fat = 4		

Honey-Glazed Carrots

If baby carrots are not available, substitute regular carrots, cut in half lengthwise and into 2-inch lengths.

1 ½ pounds baby carrots   *1 tablespoon chopped fresh cilantro*
1 teaspoon ground coriander   *½ cup honey*

Wash and scrub the carrots. Place them in a saucepan with about 5 cups of water and heat to a boil. Cook the carrots for about 20 minutes over medium heat (do not overcook; the texture of the carrots should be slightly firm). Preheat oven to 375°F. Drain and place carrots in a casserole dish. Sprinkle the coriander and cilantro and pour the honey over the carrots. Bake about 15 minutes or until the carrots are soft and slightly brown in color. *Serves 6.*

Nutritional information per serving:

calories = 100	carbohydrate = 24g	cholesterol = 0mg
sodium = 27mg	protein = 1g	fat = <1g
calories from fat = 4		

Hot and Spicy String Beans

This recipe calls for jalapeño peppers, but if you want a hotter result, try red hot chili peppers.

2 pounds fresh string beans
½ cup sliced white mushrooms
1 fresh jalapeño pepper, seeded and
    chopped
1 teaspoon freshly ground black
    pepper

1 teaspoon crushed red pepper flakes
nonstick cooking spray
2 tablespoons balsamic vinegar

Wash the beans and pat dry with a towel. Put the beans, mushrooms, jalapeño pepper, black pepper, and red pepper flakes in a large frying pan sprayed with cooking spray. Sauté over a low heat for about 10 minutes. Add the vinegar and continue to cook for another 5 minutes, or until the beans are tender but still bright green. *Serves 8.*

Nutritional information per serving:

calories = 160	carbohydrate = 30g	cholesterol = 0mg
sodium = 40mg	protein = 8g	fat = 1g
calories from fat = 9		

Green Peppers Stuffed with Black-Eyed Peas and Smoked Turkey

While this recipe calls for baking the stuffed peppers in the oven, you can also grill the stuffed peppers on a barbecue grill.

6 large green bell peppers
1 pound cooked black-eyed peas
1 cup diced smoked turkey breast
3 tablespoons diced onion

2 tablespoons diced carrot
1 teaspoon Soul Food Seasoning
  (see page 123)
½ teaspoon dried thyme powder

Cut the top off of each pepper. Remove the seeds and pulp, wash well, drain, and set aside. Mix the peas, turkey, onion, carrots, Soul Food Seasoning, and thyme in a bowl. Preheat oven to 375°F. Stuff each pepper with the mixture. Place the stuffed peppers on a nonstick cookie sheet and bake 40 minutes or until the stuffing inside the peppers is brown and firm. If more moisture is desired, cover with foil. *Serves 6.*

Nutritional information per serving:

calories = 175	carbohydrate = 24g	cholesterol = 32mg
sodium = 27mg	protein = 19g	fat = <1g
calories from fat = 5		

Macaroni and Cheese

For a creamier texture, add some nonfat mayonnaise along with the cheese and milk.

2 cups elbow macaroni
½ cup grated reduced-fat cheddar
   cheese
⅓ cup skim milk

2 tablespoons sliced scallions
1 egg white, lightly beaten
2 tablespoons nonfat Parmesan
   cheese topping

Cook the macaroni according to package instructions, and drain. Place the macaroni in a large bowl and add the cheddar cheese, milk, scallions, and egg white. Stir well. Preheat oven to 375°F. Place the macaroni in a nonstick casserole pan and sprinkle the Parmesan cheese on top. Bake about 25 minutes or until the top is browned and firm. *Serves 6.*

Nutritional information per serving:

calories = 155	carbohydrate = 27g	cholesterol = 0mg
sodium = 115mg	protein = 9g	fat = <1g
calories from fat = 5		

Spinach, Shrimp, and Eggs

This side dish can also be prepared as a breakfast meal. If you wish, try adding some chopped fresh white mushrooms.

2 pounds fresh spinach, rinsed well,
    drained, and chopped
2 teaspoons minced fresh garlic
2 egg whites, lightly beaten
½ cup small shrimp, cleaned,
    deveined, tails removed

1 tablespoon fresh lemon juice
1 teaspoon crushed red pepper flakes
½ teaspoon freshly ground black
    pepper

Sauté the spinach and garlic in a nonstick pan. Drain off juice. Pour the egg whites over the spinach. Add the shrimp, lemon juice, red pepper flakes, and black pepper, and cook another 10 minutes while constantly stirring on a low-medium heat or until the shrimp turns pink. *Serves 4.*

Nutritional information per serving:

calories = 90	carbohydrate = 9g	cholesterol = 55mg
sodium = 270mg	protein = 14g	fat = 1g
calories from fat = 11		

Wild Rice with Broccoli

Cauliflower and carrots can be used as additional ingredients in this recipe.

1 cup wild rice, rinsed well with cold water

1 cup finely chopped broccoli

¼ cup diced green bell pepper

¼ cup diced yellow bell pepper

¼ cup diced red bell pepper

½ tablespoon Soul Food Seasoning (see page 123)

Bring 2 to 2 1/2 cups water to a boil and add the rice. Reduce the heat and simmer for about 35 minutes. Add the vegetables and seasonings and cook 10 minutes longer or until the vegetables are just tender. *Serves 4.*

Nutritional information per serving:

calories = 130	carbohydrate = 28g	cholesterol = 0mg
sodium = 16mg	protein = 4g	fat = 1g
calories from fat = 9		

Mushroom Rice

Fresh oregano, thyme, and shiitake mushrooms can be used as alternatives to broccoli, marjoram, and Portobello mushrooms.

1 cup long-grain rice
nonstick cooking spray
1 ½ cups chopped Portobello
  mushrooms
¼ cup chopped scallions
2 tablespoons fresh lemon juice
1 tablespoon finely chopped fresh
  marjoram

1 tablespoon finely chopped fresh
  parsley
1 teaspoon ground white pepper
1 teaspoon Soul Food Seasoning
  (see page 123)

Pour the rice in a saucepan sprayed with nonstick cooking spray and cook stirring frequently on a low heat for about 3 minutes. Add 3 cups of water and the mushrooms. Cover and cook for about 20 minutes on a low heat or until all the liquid has been absorbed and the rice is tender. Stir in the scallions, lemon juice, marjoram, parsley, white pepper, and Soul Food Seasoning. Let stand, covered, for 3 to 5 minutes before serving. *Serves 4.*

Nutritional information per serving:

calories = 70
sodium = 8mg
calories from fat = 9

carbohydrate = 15g
protein = 2g

cholesterol = 0mg
fat = 1g

Succotash

Succotash is a word that comes from the Narragansett Indians (Native Americans from New England). It means "broken into bits." Today the word succotash means a mix of lima beans, corn, and bacon grease. This recipe is a healthier version that consists of turkey breast and other alternative seasonings.

1 cup cooked corn
1 cup cooked lima beans
½ cup precooked chopped skinless
   turkey breast
½ cup chopped onion

½ cup chopped fresh okra
2 teaspoons Soul Food Seasoning
   (see page 123)
1 teaspoon ground white pepper

Place the corn, beans, turkey, onion, okra, Soul Food Seasoning, and pepper in a saucepan. Add 2 cups of water and simmer over a low heat for about 20 minutes. *Serves 6.*

Nutritional information per serving:

calories = 200	carbohydrate = 31g	cholesterol = 32mg
sodium = 33mg	protein = 17g	fat = 2g
calories from fat = 16		

Baked Squash

This dish is even more delicious when it is served with nonfat sour cream.

¼ cup reduced-fat margarine
½ cup chopped green bell pepper
½ cup chopped celery
1 cup chopped onion

2 pounds yellow summer squash, sliced ¼-inch thick
1 teaspoon dried rosemary

Preheat the oven to 350°F. Place the margarine in a large baking casserole dish and melt in the oven. Remove the margarine from the oven and add the vegetables. Sprinkle the rosemary on top. Cover the casserole dish and bake the vegetables for about 30 minutes or until the vegetables are tender. Stir once or twice while baking. *Makes 6 servings.*

Nutritional information per serving:

calories = 81
sodium = 98mg
calories from fat = 40

carbohydrate = 11g
protein = 2g

cholesterol = 0mg
fat = 4g

Stewed Okra and Tomatoes

This recipe can be eaten alone or served over cooked rice, pasta, or beans.

2 slices turkey bacon

2 cups chopped onion

1 cup chopped green bell pepper

2 cups okra, sliced ½-inch thick

3 cups peeled and chopped tomatoes

½ teaspoon thyme

½ teaspoon freshly ground black pepper

Brown the turkey bacon in a nonstick skillet over medium-high heat, then remove from skillet. Saute the onion and green pepper until tender, then add the okra, tomatoes, thyme, and black pepper. Crumble or cut the bacon and add to the okra mixture. Cover the skillet and cook on low heat for 30 minutes. Uncover and cook for 5 minutes longer and serve. *Makes 6 servings.*

Nutritional information per serving:

calories = 83

sodium = 34mg

calories from fat = 15

carbohydrate = 16g

protein = 4g

cholesterol = 3mg

fat = 2g

Desserts

Mississippi Mud Cake

This cake has enjoyed tremendous popularity among African-American families. It is delicious, but when prepared with traditional ingredients such as pecans, whole milk, and butter, it can be remarkably high in calories, cholesterol, and fat. This version trims almost all of the sin out of the indulgence.

nonstick cooking spray
3 tablespoons cocoa
1 ½ cups mashed banana
1 cup sugar
½ cup skim milk

2 ½ cups all-purpose flour, sifted
1 ½ teaspoons baking powder
6 egg whites, lightly beaten
2 teaspoons vanilla extract
2 cups Grape Nuts Flakes

Preheat oven to 375°F. Lightly coat a nonstick 10-inch tube pan with cooking spray. In a large bowl, mix the cocoa, banana, sugar, and milk. Using an electric mixer, mix in the flour, baking powder, and egg whites, alternately. Stir in the vanilla and Grape Nuts with a large spoon. Pour the cake batter into the pan and bake about 1 hour or until cake springs back when lightly touched. Cool in pan on wire rack 10 minutes. Remove from pan and cool completely. *Serves 12.*

Nutritional information per serving:

calories = 230	carbohydrate = 48g	cholesterol = 1mg
sodium = 80mg	protein = 6g	fat = 2g
calories from fat = 14		

Allspice Applesauce Cake

This cake is low in fat because applesauce, instead of whole milk or butter, is used to keep it moist. It can be served with fresh strawberries or blueberries and nonfat whipping cream.

2 cups unsweetened applesauce
½ cup sugar
6 egg whites, at room temperature
3 cups all-purpose flour, sifted

1 ½ teaspoons baking powder
2 ½ teaspoons allspice
1 teaspoon vanilla extract
nonstick cooking spray

Preheat oven to 350°F. Using an electric mixer, beat 1 cup of applesauce with the sugar. Beat in the egg whites, one at a time. Add the flour, baking powder, allspice, and vanilla extract. Mix well. With a wooden spoon, stir in the remaining cup of applesauce until all the lumps are gone. Pour the batter into a nonstick 10-inch tube pan (or one sprayed with cooking spray). Bake about 90 minutes, or until an inserted toothpick comes out clean. Cool the cake for about 10 minutes before removing it from the pan. Let the cake cool for about half an hour before serving. *Serves 12.*

Nutritional information per serving:

calories = 180
sodium = 57mg
calories from fat = 4

carbohydrate = 39g
protein = 5g

cholesterol = 0mg
fat = <1g

Black Russian Cake

This recipe uses walnuts. Nuts are high in unsaturated fat, but not in saturated fat, too much of which can contribute to coronary heart disease. Another good thing about nuts, aside from the fact that they taste good, is that they have no cholesterol.

2 ½ cups all-purpose flour, sifted
¾ cup sugar
1 teaspoon baking soda
½ cup mashed banana
4 teaspoons cocoa
1 teaspoon vanilla extract
4 large egg whites, at room
   temperature, lightly beaten

½ cup skim milk
½ cup strong freshly brewed coffee
½ cup Kahlúa
¼ cup chopped walnuts
nonstick cooking spray

Preheat oven to 325°F. Sift the flour, sugar, and baking soda together into a large mixing bowl. In a separate bowl, thoroughly mix the banana, cocoa, and vanilla together. Add banana mixture to the flour mixture. With a wooden spoon, stir in the egg whites, skim milk, coffee, and Kahlúa. Spread the walnuts in the bottom of a nonstick 10-inch tube pan (or one sprayed with cooking spray). Pour the batter into the pan and bake about 1 1/2 hours or until an inserted toothpick comes out clean. Cool in pan on wire rack 10 minutes. Remove from pan and cool completely. *Serves 12.*

Nutritional information per serving:

calories = 220	carbohydrate = 40g	cholesterol = 0mg
sodium = 132mg	protein = 5g	fat = 2g
calories from fat = 21		

Untraditional Pound Cake

This hefty nonfat, cholesterol-free cake rivals any pound cake made with butter, whole milk, and lots of sugar.

1 ½ cups mashed bananas
¾ cup sugar
1 cup skim milk
3 cups all-purpose flour, sifted

2 teaspoons baking powder
8 egg whites, lightly beaten
1 tablespoon vanilla extract
nonstick cooking spray

Using an electric mixer, cream the bananas, sugar, and milk. Add the flour, baking powder, and egg whites alternately. Add the vanilla extract and continue to mix well. Pour the cake batter in a nonstick 10-inch tube pan (or one sprayed with cooking spray) and let set for about 10 minutes. Preheat oven to 375°F. Bake about 1 1/2 hours or until the cake turns golden brown and a toothpick inserted into the cake comes out clean. Cool in pan on wire rack for 10 minutes. Remove from pan and cool completely. *Serves 12.*

Nutritional information per serving:

calories = 200
sodium = 76mg
calories from fat = 4

carbohydrate = 41g
protein = 6.4g

cholesterol = 0mg
fat = <1g

Lemon Pound Cake

Although lemon is a great flavor in pound cake, other fruity extracts and preserves such as mango, orange, and peach may be used instead of the lemon extract and preserves.

1 cup sugar
1 cup unsweetened applesauce
4 egg whites, at room temperature
2 tablespoons lemon extract
3 cups all-purpose flour, sifted
1 ½ cups skim milk

1 ½ teaspoons baking powder
2 teaspoons lemon zest
½ cup all-natural lemon preserves
*   (no sugar added)*
nonstick cooking spray

Preheat oven to 350°F. with an electric mixer, beat the sugar and applesauce. Mix in the egg whites and lemon extract. Add the flour and milk alternately, using the flour first and last. Mix in the baking powder. Pour the cake batter into a 10-inch tube pan (or one sprayed with cooking spray) and bake about 1 1/2 hours. Remove the cake from the pan and let it cool for about 20 minutes. Heat the lemon zest and lemon preserves in a saucepan for about 1 minute (until melted enough to pour) and drizzle over the cake. *Serves 12.*

Nutritional information per serving:

calories = 215
sodium = 56mg
calories from fat = 4

carbohydrate = 29g
protein = 4g

cholesterol = 0mg
fat = <1g

Jelly Cake

A jelly cake certainly isn't a high-style dessert, but it's an old traditional delight that always seems to make a regal finish to a good soul food dinner.

1 cup sugar
1 cup mashed banana
2 ½ cups all-purpose flour, sifted
2 teaspoons baking powder
2 teaspoons vanilla extract

6 egg whites, lightly beaten
nonstick cooking spray
½ cup all-natural raspberry
preserves (no sugar added)

Preheat oven to 350°F. In a large bowl, cream the sugar and banana with an electric mixer. Then slowly mix in the flour, baking powder, and vanilla extract. Mix in the egg whites one at a time. Pour the cake batter into a nonstick 10-inch tube pan (or one sprayed with cooking spray) and bake about 1 hour or until an inserted toothpick comes out clean. Let cool for 20 minutes, then remove the cake from the pan. In a saucepan, over low heat, heat the preserves until melted enough to pour, stirring constantly about one minute. Drizzle the preserves over the cake and serve. *Serves 12.*

Nutritional information per serving:

calories = 210	carbohydrate = 47g	cholesterol = 0mg
sodium = 57mg	protein = 4g	fat = <1g
calories from fat = 3		

Banana Pudding

This recipe is dedicated to my mother, who could make an awesome banana pudding the traditional way (which includes egg yolks, lots of sugar, and evaporated whole milk). This revised version is just as tasty but much healthier.

¼ cup sugar
2 tablespoons cornstarch
2 cups evaporated skim milk
2 teaspoons vanilla extract
2 ½ cups vanilla wafer crumbs

3 cups bananas, sliced
5 large egg whites, at room
* temperature*
ground cinnamon

Preheat oven to 400°F. Combine the sugar, cornstarch, and milk in a medium saucepan. Cook over a low heat, stirring constantly until the mixture thickens like pudding. Add the vanilla extract. In a 9-inch or 10-inch casserole dish, arrange a layer of vanilla wafers (touching each other). Arrange a layer of banana slices on top of the wafers. Repeat with wafers and bananas. Pour the thickened pudding mixture over the bananas. Using an electric mixer, beat the egg whites until stiff, then spread on top of the pudding. Sprinkle cinnamon on top. Bake the pudding until the surface of the egg whites begins to brown. Let the custard cool for about 2 hours before serving. *Serves 8.*

Nutritional information per serving:

calories = 200
sodium = 129mg
calories from fat = 33

carbohydrate = 35g
protein = 7g

cholesterol = 14mg
fat = 4g

Bread Pudding

Either white or whole wheat bread can be used for this recipe. For the ultimate bread pudding, a delicious Honey Rum-Raisin Sauce is recommended as a topping (recipe follows).

12 whole wheat bread slices, toasted
   and cut into ½-inch cubes
1 ½ cups skim milk
¼ cup sugar
¼ cup golden raisins

2 egg whites, lightly beaten
2 teaspoons vanilla extract
2 teaspoons ground cinnamon
½ teaspoon ground cardamom

Preheat oven to 375°F. Place the bread cubes in a large bowl and soak them in the milk. Sprinkle the sugar on top of the bread. In a separate bowl, combine raisins, egg whites, vanilla, cinnamon, and cardamom. Mix thoroughly and pour over the bread cubes. Pour entire mixture into a 1 1/2- or 2-quart casserole baking dish. Place the casserole dish in a larger baking pan. Add water to come up 1 inch of the casserole. Bake about 20 to 30 minutes until the pudding is golden brown and firm. It can be served right out of the oven or served cold by refrigerating it for about 3 hours (covered with plastic wrap). *Serves 6.*

Nutritional information per serving:

calories = 115	carbohydrate = 26g	cholesterol = 0mg
sodium = 147mg	protein = 4g	fat = 1g
calories from fat = 5		

Honey Rum-Raisin Sauce

For a rich, sweet accompaniment to the Bread Pudding, prepare this Honey Rum-Raisin Sauce. Drizzle it over each serving of bread pudding.

½ cup dark rum

½ cup honey

¼ cup water

¼ cup dark raisins

Combine the rum, honey, water, and raisins in a saucepan and simmer for 5 minutes over a low to medium heat, stirring continuously until the sauce thickens. *Makes about 1 cup.*

Nutritional information per tablespoon:

calories = 26	carbohydrate = 2g	cholesterol = 0mg
sodium = 0g	protein = 0g	fat = 0g
calories from fat = 0		

Peach Cobbler

You can substitute other fruits such as plums or strawberries for the peaches in this cobbler.

1½ cups all-purpose flour	1 teaspoon ground cloves
1 cup skim milk	1 teaspoon grated nutmeg
2 egg whites	3 cups fresh peaches, sliced
¾ cup honey	1 teaspoon ground cinnamon

Preheat oven to 375°F. Mix the flour, milk, and egg whites together. Pour the honey, cloves, and nutmeg over the peaches and stir well. Place the peaches in a 9-inch casserole baking dish and pour the flour mixture on top of the peaches. Sprinkle the cinnamon on top. Do not stir. Bake about 40 minutes or until the top browns. This cobbler can be served right out of the oven or served chilled by placing it in the refrigerator for about 3 hours (covered with plastic wrap). *Makes 6 servings.*

Nutritional information per serving:

calories = 220	carbohydrate = 51g	cholesterol = 1mg
sodium = 42mg	protein = 5g	fat = <1g
calories from fat = 5		

Coconut-Banana Pie

Although coconut is high in saturated fat, it is a plant and so contains no cholesterol. Coconut pies freeze very well—any uneaten portions may be wrapped and kept in the freezer for 2 to 3 months. This recipe calls for a pie shell (see page 111); however, the coconut-banana filling can be prepared alone and eaten as a dessert without the pie shell.

½ cup sugar
½ cup mashed banana
3 egg whites, lightly beaten
½ cup evaporated skim milk

1 cup shredded fresh coconut
1 teaspoon ground cinnamon
1 9-inch Reduced-Fat Pie Shell (see
  page 111)

Preheat oven to 350°F. Using an electric mixer, beat the sugar and banana together until slightly fluffy. Using a large spoon, stir in the egg whites, skim milk, coconut, and cinnamon, blending thoroughly. Pour the pie filling into the pie shell, and bake about 45 minutes to 1 hour or until firm. *Serves 8 to 10.*

Nutritional information per serving:

calories = 190	carbohydrate = 33g	cholesterol = 1mg
sodium = 187mg	protein = 4g	fat = 5g
calories from fat = 45		

Old-Fashioned Egg Custard

This recipe can also be made with reconstituted dried fruits, such as cherries, pears, or apples.

1 cup skim milk
1/4 cup sugar
2 teaspoons vanilla extract
10 egg whites
1/4 cup mashed banana

2 teaspoons ground cinnamon
1 teaspoon grated nutmeg
1/2 teaspoon ground cloves
1 9-inch Reduced-Fat Pie Shell (see page 111)

Preheat oven to 375°F. Heat the skim milk and sugar in a medium saucepan until warm, stirring constantly. Set aside. Using an electric mixer, mix the vanilla extract, egg whites, banana, cinnamon, nutmeg, and cloves for about 3 minutes or until fluffy. Add the lukewarm sugar-milk to the beaten egg whites. Pour into the pie shell and bake about 1 hour or until the custard is firm. *Serves 8.*

Nutritional information per serving:
calories = 170
sodium = 250mg
calories from fat = 18

carbohydrate = 29g
protein = 8g

cholesterol = 1mg
fat = 2g

Sweet Potato Pie

You can give sweet potato pie a special twist by adding 1/2 cup golden raisins or 1/2 cup Grape Nuts cereal to the filling before baking.

2 cups cooked sweet potatoes, peeled
¾ cup honey
4 egg whites
1 ½ cups skim milk
1 teaspoon grated nutmeg
½ teaspoon ground cinnamon

½ teaspoon ground mace
¼ teaspoon ground allspice
2 teaspoons fresh lemon juice
1 9-inch Reduced-Fat Pie Shell (see page 111)

Preheat oven to 375°F. With an electric mixer thoroughly blend all the ingredients together. Pour the filling into the pie shell and bake about 40 minutes or until firm. Remove the pie from the oven and allow it to cool for about 20 minutes before serving—or allow it to cool and cover it with plastic wrap and store in the refrigerator until ready to serve. *Serves 10.*

Nutritional information per serving:

calories = 170
sodium = 51mg
calories from fat = 3

carbohydrate = 39g
protein = 4g

cholesterol = 1mg
fat = <1g

Pumpkin Pie
with Golden Raisins

If pumpkin is not available, use canned solid packed pumpkin.

4 egg whites, lightly beaten
2 cups cooked pumpkin
½ cup honey
1 ½ cups evaporated skim milk
½ cup golden raisins

1 teaspoon ground cinnamon
1 teaspoon ground ginger
½ teaspoon ground cloves
1 9-inch Reduced-Fat Pie Shell (see page 111)

Preheat oven to 425°F. In a large bowl, thoroughly blend with an electric mixer all the ingredients and pour into the pie shell. Bake for about 20 minutes or until an inserted toothpick comes out clean. *Serves 8.*

Nutritional information per serving:

calories = 270	carbohydrate = 53g	cholesterol = 4mg
sodium = 249mg	protein = 9g	fat = 3g
calories from fat = 25		

Reduced-Fat Pie Shell

1 ½ cups all-purpose flour
½ teaspoon "lite" salt (optional)
3 tablespoons reduced-fat
   margarine, cold, cut into small
   pieces

3 tablespoons cold skim milk

Mix the flour and salt together in a bowl. Add the margarine, and using fingertips rub in until the flour resembles coarse crumbs. Sprinkle with skim milk and blend until the dry ingredients hold together. Using your hands, shape into a ball and wrap in plastic wrap. Refrigerate until chilled

When ready to roll out, place the dough ball on a lightly floured board and roll out to about an 1/8-inch-thick circle, rolling the dough about 2-inches larger than the pie pan. Fold the dough in half and gently place it in the pie pan. Unfold the dough and fit it to the pan, tucking an extra 1-inch of crust to make a thick stand-up edge. *Makes one 9-inch or 10-inch pie shell (8 to 10 servings).*

Nutritional information per serving:

calories = 80
sodium = 132mg
calories from fat = 13

carbohydrate = 15g
protein = 2g

cholesterol = 0mg
fat = 1g

Lemon Mousse

When serving this elegant dessert, you can place a crisp low-fat cookie or a sprig of mint atop each parfait.

3 tablespoons fresh lemon juice
2 teaspoons grated lemon rind, plus
   additional for garnish
¼ cup confectioners' sugar, sifted

2 cups of Cool Whip Lite Whipped
   Topping
2 egg whites, beaten stiff

Combine the lemon juice, rind, sugar, and whipped cream in a large bowl. Fold in the beaten egg whites just until blended. Fill parfait glasses with the mousse and freeze. Keep frozen until ready to serve. Some additional lemon rind may be sprinkled on top for garnish. Serves 4.

Nutritional information per serving:

calories = 120	carbohydrate = 16g	cholesterol = 0mg
sodium = 28mg	protein = 2g	fat = 4g
calories from fat = 36		

Cranberry Ice

A Raspberry-Cranberry flavored ice can be made by adding 1/4 cup of fresh raspberries to this recipe.

1 48-ounce jar of natural cranberry   *sprigs of mint, for garnish*
    cocktail drink
½ cup fresh or frozen cranberries
    (slightly mashed)

Combine the cranberry juice and fresh cranberries, and pour in an ice cream maker. Freeze according to manufacturer's directions. Scoop out the frozen dessert into stemmed dessert glasses and garnish with sprigs of fresh mint. *Serves 12 (2 scoops per serving)*.

Nutritional information per serving:

calories = 70	carbohydrate = 18g	cholesterol = 0mg
sodium = 5mg	protein = 0g	fat = <1g
calories from fat = 1		

Watermelon Sherbet

This seasonal recipe is a refreshing treat during the summer months.

6 cups fresh sweet watermelon, seeds
removed
¼ cup peeled and sliced fresh peach
¼ cup peeled and sliced fresh Red
Delicious apple

¼ cup peeled and sliced fresh pear
sprigs of fresh mint, for garnish

Place the watermelon, peach, apple, and pear in an electric blender, and purée. Pour the purée into an ice cream maker and freeze as manufacturer directs. Scoop out into dessert bowls and garnish with sprigs of mint. *Makes about 6 servings.*

Nutritional information per serving:

calories = 60
sodium = 2mg
calories from fat = 7

carbohydrate = 14g
protein = 1g

cholesterol = 0mg
fat = <1g

Fresh Fruit Salad

When seasonal fruits are not available, frozen fruits can be used to make this recipe. Chopped fresh mint can be added for a surprising flavor. This salad can also be served as a topping for a Lemon Pound Cake (see page 93).

1 cup cubed pineapple
1 cup sliced strawberries
1 cup seedless grapes
1 cup sliced banana

1 cup raspberries
3 tablespoons honey
1 tablespoon fresh lemon juice

Combine all the fruit in a large bowl. Stir the honey and lemon juice together in a small bowl and pour over the fruit. Stir. Chill the salad in the refrigerator for about 3 hours before serving, so that the flavors meld. *Serves 6.*

Nutritional information per serving:

calories = 90
sodium = 2mg
calories from fat = 4

carbohydrate = 23g
protein = 1g

cholesterol = 0mg
fat = <1g

Rice Pudding

The Honey Rum-Raisin Sauce on page 105 can be served with this Rice Pudding recipe.

¼ cup long-grain white rice
½ cup boiling water
2 cups skim milk
2 tablespoons reduced-fat
   margarine

¼ cup sugar
¼ cup freshly grated orange zest
2 egg whites, beaten slightly stiff
¼ teaspoon ground cinnamon

Combine the rice and boiling water in a saucepan. Cover and bring to a boil, then reduce heat and simmer for 10 minutes or until rice is almost tender. Add milk and margarine. Bring to a boil again, then reduce heat and simmer uncovered 10 minutes longer, stirring often. Stir in the sugar and orange zest. Remove 1 cup of the rice mixture, stir the egg white into it, then return it to the saucepan with the rest of the rice mixture and cook and stir for 1 minute. Cool the pudding for about 10 minutes. Scoop the rice pudding into 5-ounce dessert glasses, sprinkle with cinnamon and serve warm, or refrigerate for 1 hour and serve cold. *Serves 4 to 6.*

Nutritional information per serving:

calories = 136
sodium = 113mg
calories from fat = 19

carbohydrate = 24g
protein = 5g

cholesterol = 1mg
fat = 2g

Date Nut Squares

These delicious squares can be served with a reduced-fat vanilla ice cream.

1 cup dates	*1 ½ cups all-purpose flour*
1 teaspoon baking soda	*1 teaspoon cocoa powder*
1 cup boiling water	*1 teaspoon vanilla extract*
¼ cup reduced-fat margarine	*¼ cup chopped pecans*
¼ cup sugar	*¼ cup semisweet chocolate chips*

Preheat the oven to 350°F. Cut up the dates with kitchen scissors and place them in a bowl. Sprinkle the dates with baking soda, add boiling water, and set aside. Place the margarine and sugar in a medium bowl and cream with an electric mixer until the texture is light and fluffly. Gradually stir in the flour, cocoa, and vanilla. Add the date mixture and mix well. Spread the dough in a nonstick 13 x 9-inch baking pan. Sprinkle pecans and chocolate chips over the top. Bake for 40 minutes or until a toothpick inserted in the center comes out clean. Remove from the oven and let cool for 10 minutes. Cut into small rectangles or squares. *Makes about 12 servings.*

Nutritional information per serving:

calories = 183	carbohydrate = 32g	cholesterol = 0mg
sodium = 74mg	protein = 3g	fat = 6g
calories from fat = 51		

Sour Cream Cookies

Instead of the black currants used in this recipe, 1/4 cup of finely chopped pecans can be substituted.

2 cups all-purpose flour
1 ½ teaspoons baking powder
½ cup reduced-fat margarine
½ cup sugar
2 egg whites, slightly beaten

½ cup light sour cream
½ cup dried currants
½ teaspoon cinnamon (for topping)
1 tablespoon sugar (for topping)

Preheat the oven to 400°F. Sift the flour and baking powder together, place in a mixing bowl, and set aside. In a separate mixing bowl cream the margarine and sugar with an electric mixer until the texture turns light and fluffy. Add the egg whites and continue to mix until well mixed. Add the flour mix alternately with the sour cream; beat until smooth after each addition. Stir in the currants. Drop dough by rounded teaspoonfuls spaced 1 1/2-inches apart onto a nonstick cookie sheet. Press each cookie somewhat flat with the bottom of a glass dipped in additional sugar. Sprinkle the top of the cookies with 1/2 teaspoon of cinnamon and 1 tablespoon sugar mixed together. Bake for 10 to 12 minutes or until the top and edges of cookies turn golden brown. *Makes 3 dozen.*

Nutritional information per serving:

calories = 137	carbohydrate = 24g	cholesterol = 1mg
sodium = 113mg	protein = 3g	fat = 3g
calories from fat = 31		

Sauces, Seasonings, and Dips

Citrus Barbecue Sauce

This tangy, savory sauce can be served with appetizers such as African-American Meatballs (see page 10), Baked Chicken Strips (see page 13), and Fried Green Tomatoes (see page 4), or with main dishes such as Unfried Chicken (see page 65).

½ cup finely diced onion
¼ cup finely diced lemon rind
1 tablespoon fresh lemon juice
½ cup fresh orange juice
¼ cup honey

½ cup ketchup
½ cup water
1 teaspoon dry mustard
½ teaspoon ground white pepper

Combine all the ingredients in a small saucepan and bring to a boil, stirring constantly. Reduce heat and simmer for about 5 minutes. *Makes about 2 cups.*

Nutritional information per 2 tablespoons:

calories = 32
sodium = 102mg
calories from fat = 1

carbohydrate = 8g
protein = 0g

cholesterol = 0mg
fat = <1g

Herbal Barbecue Sauce

This sauce works well with appetizers such as Baked Chicken Strips (see page 13), Fried Okra (see page 3), and Sweet Potato Chips (see page 6); entrees such as Stuffed Pork Tenderloin with Vegetables (see page 72); or side dishes such as Fried Turkey and Rice (see page 82) and Homemade Fries (see page 84).

1 tablespoon finely chopped fresh marjoram

1 tablespoon finely chopped fresh rosemary

1 tablespoon finely chopped fresh sage

¼ cup cider vinegar

1 teaspoon freshly ground black pepper

½ cup ketchup

½ cup water

⅓ cup honey

1 teaspoon mustard powder

Combine all the ingredients in a small saucepan and bring to a boil, stirring constantly. Reduce heat and simmer for about 5 minutes. *Makes about 2 cups.*

Nutritional information per 2 tablespoons:

calories = 31	carbohydrate = 8g	cholesterol = 0mg
sodium = 102mg	protein = 0g	fat = <1g
calories from fat = 1		

Soul Food Seasoning

If you want to keep a greater quantity of this useful seasoning on hand, simply double or triple the quantities.

1 tablespoon ground red pepper
3 tablespoons garlic powder
3 tablespoons onion powder
1 tablespoon dark chili powder

1 tablespoon paprika
1 teaspoon thyme powder
1 teaspoon freshly ground black
*   pepper*

Mix all the ingredients together. Store in a sealed container. *Makes about 3/4 cup.*

Nutritional information per 1/2 teaspoon:

calories = 5
sodium = 3mg
calories from fat = 1

carbohydrate = 1g
protein = 0g

cholesterol = 0mg
fat = <1g

Nonfat Cucumber Dip

This dip can be served with breads such as Tomato Bread (see page 22) or Herb Rolls (see page 25).

½ cup nonfat plain yogurt
⅓ cup minced fresh cucumber
2 tablespoons fresh lemon juice

1 ½ teaspoons chopped fresh dill
1 ½ teaspoons chopped fresh
    tarragon

Combine all the ingredients in a bowl, stirring thoroughly. Cover and chill in the refrigerator for at least 3 hours before serving. *Makes about 1 cup.*

Nutritional information per tablespoon:

calories = 5
sodium = 5mg
calories from fat = 0

carbohydrate = 1g
protein = 0g

cholesterol = 0mg
fat = 0g

Nonfat Spinach Dip

This dip can be served with appetizers such as Fried Okra (see page 3), Stuffed Mushrooms Wrapped in Turkey Bacon (see page 11), or Baked Chicken Strips (see page 13).

1 cup cooked spinach
⅓ cup fat-free cottage cheese
⅓ cup sliced green onion

2 tablespoons fresh lemon juice
2 tablespoons nonfat mayonnaise
2 tablespoons fresh chopped garlic

Place all the ingredients in a blender or food processor and mix until smooth. Spoon into a bowl. Cover and chill in the refrigerator for at least 3 hours, to allow flavors to develop, before serving. *Makes 2 cups.*

Nutritional information per 2 tablespoons:

calories = 10	carbohydrate = 2g	cholesterol = 0mg
sodium = 35mg	protein = 1g	fat = 0g
calories from fat = 0		

Low-Carb
Recipes

Smoked Salmon Salad

Smoked trout can be used instead of smoked salmon, and less expensive chopped iceberg lettuce can be substituted for the field greens.

4 cups (6 ounces) ready to eat
*   packaged field greens*
2 ounces boneless smoked salmon
1 teaspoon extra virgin olive oil

2 tablespoons chopped pecans
2 tablespoons raisins
1/2 teaspoon freshly ground black
*   pepper*

Place the field greens into two salad bowls. Using a fork, flake the salmon into 1/2-inch pieces and place on top of the field greens. Sprinkle half of the remaining ingredients into each of the salads bowls. Chill for about 1 hour and serve. *Makes 2 servings.*

Nutritional information per serving:

calories = 150	carbohydrate = 14g	cholesterol = 7mg
sodium = 234mg	protein = 8g	fat = 8g
calories from fat = 76		

Egg Salad

Roasted chicken (about 1/2 cup, boneless, skinless and diced) can be added to this recipe. And, it can be served over 1 cup coarsely chopped lettuce.

6 hard-boiled eggs, peeled
¼ cup low-fat mayonnaise
¼ cup diced celery
¼ cup diced onions

½ tablespoon Dijon mustard
1 teaspoon pickle relish
¼ teaspoon sweet paprika
  (for topping)

Cut the eggs in half. Discard the yolks from 4 of the eggs. Chop the remainder of the eggs and place in a medium-size bowl. Stir in the rest of the ingredients, sprinkle with paprika and chill about 2 hours before serving. *Makes 4 servings.*

Nutritional information per serving:

calories = 106	carbohydrate = 4g	cholesterol = 107mg
sodium = 265mg	protein = 7g	fat = 7g
calories from fat = 59		

Spicy Corn Cakes (Appetizer)

1 cup fresh corn, cut from the cob
   (about 2 ears)
¼ cup all-purpose flour
½ teaspoon garlic powder

¼ teaspoon white pepper
2 egg whites, slightly beaten
Nonstick cooking spray

Place 1/2 cup of the corn kernels and the remainder of the ingredients into a food processor. Blend 1 minute on high speed. Add the other half of the corn kernels to the blended mixture and set aside. Coat a large skillet with cooking spray and heat over medium heat until hot; spoon one tablespoon of the corn mixture into a frying pan. Cook corn 1 minute on each side, or until the cakes turn brown and firm. *Makes 8 pieces.*

Nutritional information per piece:

calories = 19
sodium = 14mg
calories from fat = 0

carbohydrate = 3g
protein = 1g

cholesterol = 0mg
fat = 0g

Crab Cakes (APPETIZER)

These cakes can be cooked on a grill and served with lemon wedges and barbecue sauce.

1 cup fresh crab meat
1/4 cup scallions
1/4 cup plain bread crumbs
1/2 teaspoon garlic powder
1/2 teaspoon onion powder

1/4 teaspoon Worcestershire sauce
1/4 cup low-fat mayonnaise
1 egg white, slightly beaten
Nonstick cooking spray

Combine all the ingredients in a medium-size bowl and mix well. Shape into 4 patties and chill for 2 hours. Coat a large skillet with non-stick cooking spray and heat over medium heat until hot. Place the patties into the skillet and cook for 3 minutes on each side, or until they are brown and firm. *Makes 8 pieces.*

Nutritional information per piece:

calories = 59	carbohydrate = 4g	cholesterol = 17mg
sodium = 137mg	protein = 4g	fat = 3g
calories from fat = 25		

Barbecued Shrimp (MAIN DISH)

A spicier version of this recipe can be made by adding 1 tablespoon of diced jalapeño peppers to the barbecue sauce.

2 pounds medium-size shrimp,
  peeled and cleaned
½ cup barbecue sauce

1 tablespoon freshly minced garlic
¼ cup chopped parsley,
  for garnishing

Toss the shrimp together with the barbecue sauce and garlic; cover and refrigerate about 4 hours or overnight. Put the marinated shrimp on a nonstick baking sheet; place under the broiler about 2 minutes, turn the shrimp over and broil another 2 minutes. Be sure to place the baking sheet at least 6 inches away from the heat source. *Makes 6 to 8 servings.*

Nutritional information per serving:

calories = 146	carbohydrate = 7g	cholesterol = 172mg
sodium = 400mg	protein = 23g	fat = 2g
calories from fat = 22		

Pecan-Crusted Trout (MAIN DISH)

Catfish can be substituted for the trout. And cutting up the fish into fillets makes the coating easier.

1 teaspoon garlic powder

1 teaspoon onion powder

1 teaspoon oregano

¼ teaspoon cayenne pepper

¼ teaspoon black pepper

1 cup finely chopped pecans

2 pounds trout, cleaned, cut into
* 6 to 8 fillets*

2 egg whites, slightly beaten

Nonstick cooking spray

Combine the garlic powder, onion powder, oregano, cayenne pepper, black pepper, and chopped pecans together and mix well. Dredge each piece of fillet into the coating, covering both sides, then dip into the egg whites and dredge again. Coat a large skillet with nonstick cooking spray, heat over medium heat until hot. Spray each coated fillet with cooking spray on both sides. Place each fillet in the skillet and cook 3 to 4 minutes on both sides. *Makes 6 to 8 pieces.*

Nutritional information per serving:

calories = 265	carbohydrate = 3g	cholesterol = 65mg
sodium = 73mg	protein = 26g	fat = 17g
calories from fat = 150		

Cajun Meatloaf (Main Dish)

Lean ground chicken breast or lean ground pork can be used instead of beef.

1 tablespoon canola oil	1½ pounds lean ground beef
¼ cup diced onions	1 can (14 ounces) diced tomatoes
¼ cup diced green onions (scallions)	¼ cup plain bread crumbs
¼ cup chopped button mushrooms	3 egg whites, slightly beaten
¼ cup diced celery	½ teaspoon freshly ground black pepper
¼ cup diced green bell peppers	1 teaspoon Tabasco sauce

Preheat oven to 400°F. Place canola oil in a large skillet and heat over a medium heat until hot. Add onions, green onions, mushrooms, celery, bell peppers and sauté until soft, about 4 minutes; set aside and let cool. Using a large bowl, combine the beef, tomatoes, bread crumbs, egg whites and mix well. Add the sautéed vegetables, black pepper and Tabasco sauce; continue to mix well. Place in a 7-inch loaf pan, bake in oven for 40 minutes. *Makes 6 to 8 servings.*

Nutritional information per serving:

calories = 301	carbohydrate = 7g	cholesterol = 84mg
sodium = 124mg	protein = 28g	fat = 18g
calories from fat = 159		

Orange Chicken Kebabs (Main Dish)

Beef or pork can be substituted for chicken, and lemon or lime juice can be used instead of orange juice.

1½ pounds chicken breast,
    cut into 1-inch cubes
1 tablespoon chopped garlic
1 cup orange juice
2 tablespoons orange zest
½ cup barbecue sauce
1 medium (about ¾ cup) green bell
    pepper, cut into 1-inch squares

1 medium (about ¾ cup) red bell
    pepper, cut into 1-inch squares
1 medium (about ¾ cup) yellow
    bell pepper, cut into 1-inch
    squares
8–10 skewers

Place the chicken, garlic, orange juice in a resealable plastic bag; seal and refrigerate at least 8 hours, turning occasionally. Drain, reserving about 1/4 cup of the marinade. Combine the barbecue sauce and reserve marinade in a small sauce pan and heat, stirring constantly over medium heat until boiling, about 2 minutes. Heat the grill. If using wooden skewers, soak in water for at least 15 minutes to prevent burning. Skewer the chicken and the peppers. Grill about 5 minutes on each side, or until chicken is fully cooked, brushing with some of the sauce and turning frequently. Serve the kebabs with the remaining sauce. *Makes about 8 to 10 kebabs.*

Nutritional information per kebab:
calories = 154
sodium = 239mg
calories from fat = 26
carbohydrate = 9g
protein = 22g
cholesterol = 58mg
fat = 3g

Sea Bass With Bell Pepper Sauce (Main Dish)

For a zesty flavor, add one tablespoon of lemon zest to the sauce.

4 8-ounce sea bass fillets
nonstick cooking spray
1 medium (about ¾ cup) yellow
   bell pepper, diced
1 medium (about ¾ cup) red bell
   pepper, diced

⅓ cup dry white wine
1 tablespoon freshly chopped
   basil
1 tablespoon freshly chopped
   tarragon

Preheat oven to 450°F. Place the fillets in a single layer in a large baking pan and spray both sides with nonstick cooking spray. Bake 10 minutes or until the fish turns opaque and flakes easily. Place the remaining ingredients in a food processor, and process for 1 minute; transfer to a small nonstick skillet and cook over medium heat about 3 minutes. Pour the sauce over the fillets. *Makes 4 servings.*

Nutritional information per serving:

calories = 259	carbohydrate = 6g	cholesterol = 93mg
sodium = 157mg	protein = 43mg	fat = 5g
calories from fat = 43		

Broccoli With Lemon Sauce (SIDE DISH)

Cauliflower can be substituted for the broccoli.

½ cup reduced fat mayonnaise
¼ cup fat free sour cream
1 tablespoon fresh lemon juice

1 teaspoon lemon zest
3 cups hot cooked broccoli
  florets

Combine all the ingredients except the broccoli florets, in the top of a double boiler. Cook over simmering water about 5 minutes or until heated, stirring constantly. Serve immediately over the hot cooked broccoli florets. *Makes 4 servings.*

Nutritional information per serving:

calories = 118	carbohydrate = 7g	cholesterol = 0mg
sodium = 224mg	protein = 4g	fat = 9g
calories from fat = 84		

Stir-Fried Vegetables <small>(SIDE DISH)</small>

This dish can be served with a sweet & sour sauce or a small amount of low-sodium soy sauce.

¼ cup canola oil
1 cup zucchini, cut into matchstick
strips (julienne)
1 cup carrots, cut into matchstick
strips

1 medium (¾ cup) red bell pepper,
seeded and sliced into strips
1 medium (¾ cup) yellow bell
pepper, seeded and sliced
into strips

Heat the oil in a large nonstick skillet or wok. Add the vegetables and stir fry over high heat about 4 to 5 minutes, or until they are tender. Serve immediately. *Makes 4 servings.*

Nutritional information per serving:
calories = 114
sodium = 14mg
calories from fat = 84
carbohydrate = 8g
protein = 1g
cholesterol = 0mg
fat = 9g

Roasted Veggies (Side Dish)

Flavored oils such as basil, rosemary and chili, can be used instead of olive oil.

1 cup chopped red onions
1 cup chopped yellow or white onions
1 cup zucchini, cut into 2-inch slices
1 cup eggplant, cut into 2-inch chunks
½ cup red bell pepper, seeded and diced

½ cup green bell pepper, seeded and diced
2 tablespoons chopped garlic
¼ cup extra virgin olive oil
1 tablespoon freshly chopped basil
1 tablespoon fresh thyme

Preheat the oven to 425°F. Place all the ingredients (except the oil and herbs) in a medium size nonstick roasting pan. Sprinkle the oil over the vegetables and toss well with hands. Bake 20 to 25 minutes, or until the vegetables are tender. Pour cooked vegetables on a serving platter; sprinkle fresh herbs on top and serve. *Makes 6 servings.*

Nutritional information per serving:

calories = 126	carbohydrate = 10g	cholesterol = 0mg
sodium = 5mg	protein = 2g	fat = 9g
calories from fat = 84		

Chocolate Dutch Treat (DESSERT)

This recipe can be served warm or cold. If served cold, chill in the refrigerator at least 2 hours before serving.

⅓ cup unsweetened Dutch (European style) cocoa powder	⅓ cup sugar
1 tablespoon cornstarch	1 teaspoon pure vanilla extract
1¼ cups reduced fat (2%) milk	¼ teaspoon allspice
	1 teaspoon finely chopped pecans

Place the cocoa powder and cornstarch in a small double boiler. Gradually whisk in the milk until well blended. Then, heat over medium heat for 4 minutes, stirring constantly. Stir in the sugar, vanilla, and allspice. Let stand for 5 minutes; pour into dessert bowl and sprinkle with pecans. *Makes 4 to 6 servings.*

Nutritional information per serving:

calories = 99	carbohydrate = 15g	cholesterol = 5mg
sodium = 37mg	protein = 3g	fat = 3g
calories from fat = 26		

Mixed Berry Delight (DESSERT)

If fresh seasonal berries are not available, frozen ones can be used instead. However, they must be used frozen, do not thaw them out.

1 cup fresh blackberries
1 cup fresh blueberries
1 cup fresh raspberries
1 cup fresh strawberries

¼ cup sugar
2 tablespoons lemon juice
4–6 fresh mint leaves for
   garnishing

Place all the fruit in a large bowl and set aside. Mix the sugar and lemon juice together in a cup and pour over the fruit. Stir gently with a large wooden spoon; cover and refrigerate about 1 hour before serving. Garnish with mint leaves. *Makes 6 to 8 servings.*

Nutritional information per serving:

calories = 57
sodium = 2mg
calories from fat = 3

carbohydrate = 14g
protein = 1g

cholesterol = 0mg
fat = 0g

Vanilla Cream Pudding (DESSERT)

Liquor such as bourbon or whiskey can be used instead of the vanilla extract.

⅓ cup packed light brown sugar
8 ounces fat free cream cheese,
  softened

2 teaspoons pure vanilla extract
½ teaspoon vanilla seeds, removed
  from a vanilla bean

Place the sugar and cream cheese in a medium mixing bowl. Mix with an electric mixer until smooth. Fold in the vanilla extract and seeds; cover and refrigerate about 2 to 3 hours before serving. *Makes 4 to 6 servings.*

Nutritional information per serving:

calories = 83
sodium = 231mg
calories from fat = 0

carbohydrate = 14g
protein = 5g

cholesterol = 0mg
fat = 0g

Index